Spatial Labyrinths

Spatial Labyrinths

Zoltan Homonnai

To order additional copies of this book, contact:
Xlibris Corporation
1-888-795-4274
www.Xlibris.com
Orders@Xlibris.com
100395

The children are climbing a mountain.
Who can reach the top, and who can not?
Use different colors to mark the roads.
What do you think, the shortest way is?

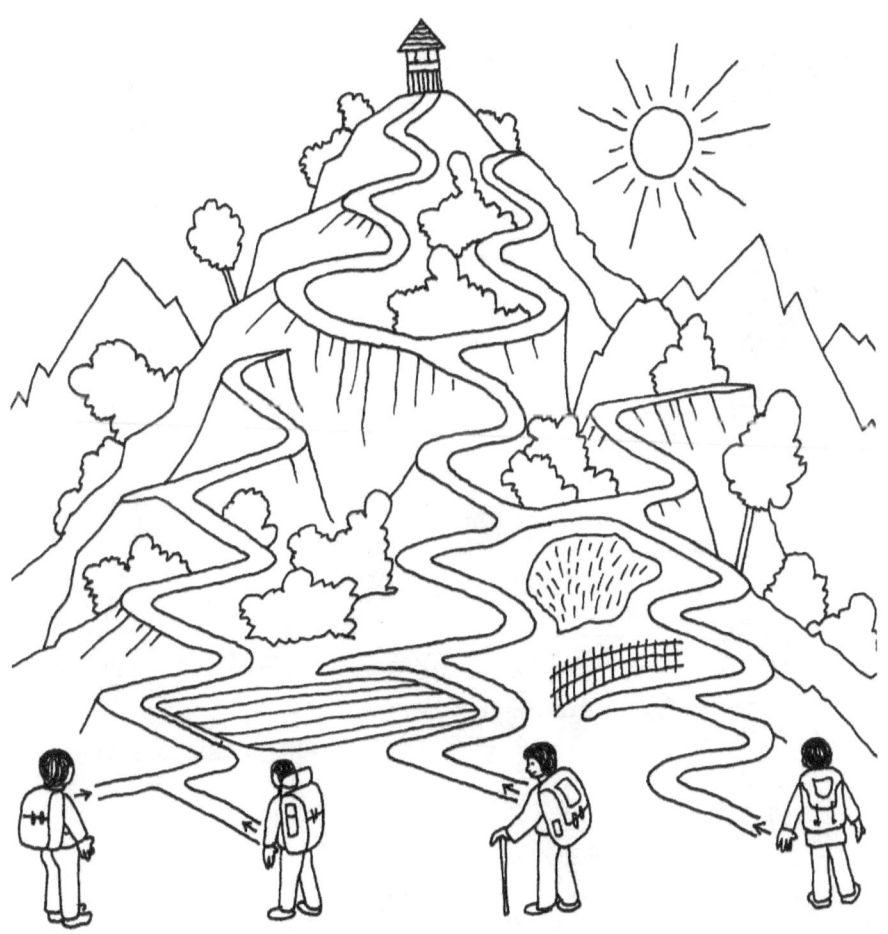

Mike would like to catch the spider.
Help him! How can he go up?
There are more solutions, how many did you find?

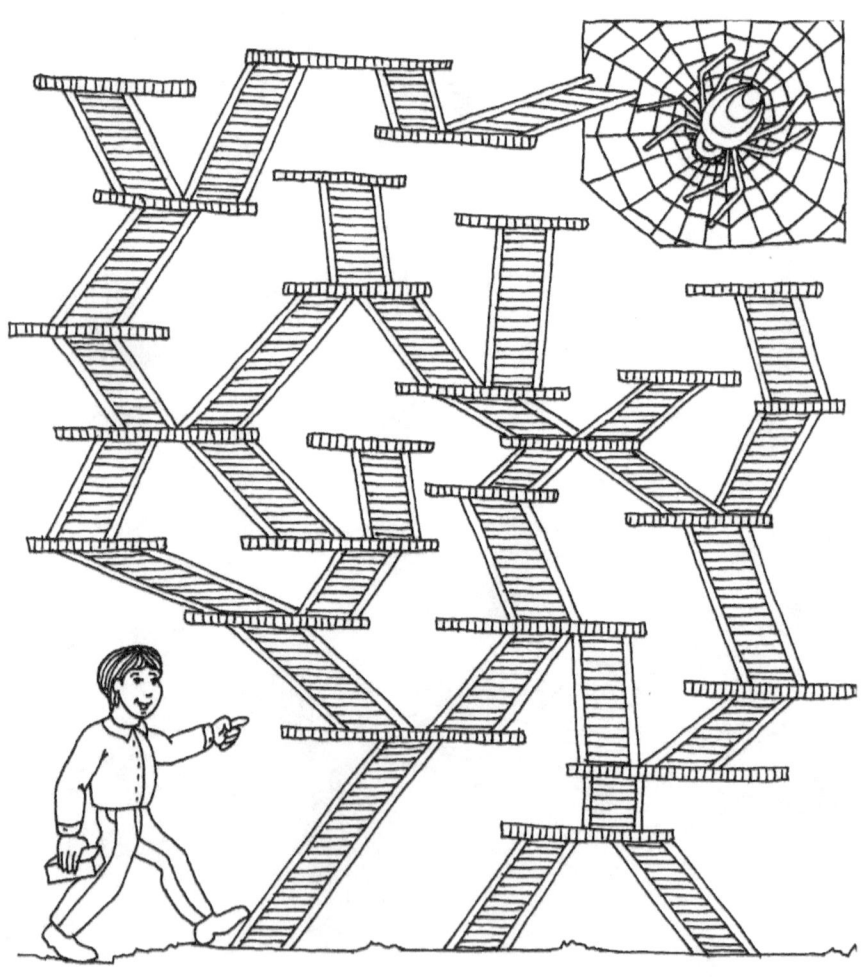

Which horse reaches the goal?
You can not hop over the fences.
Mark!

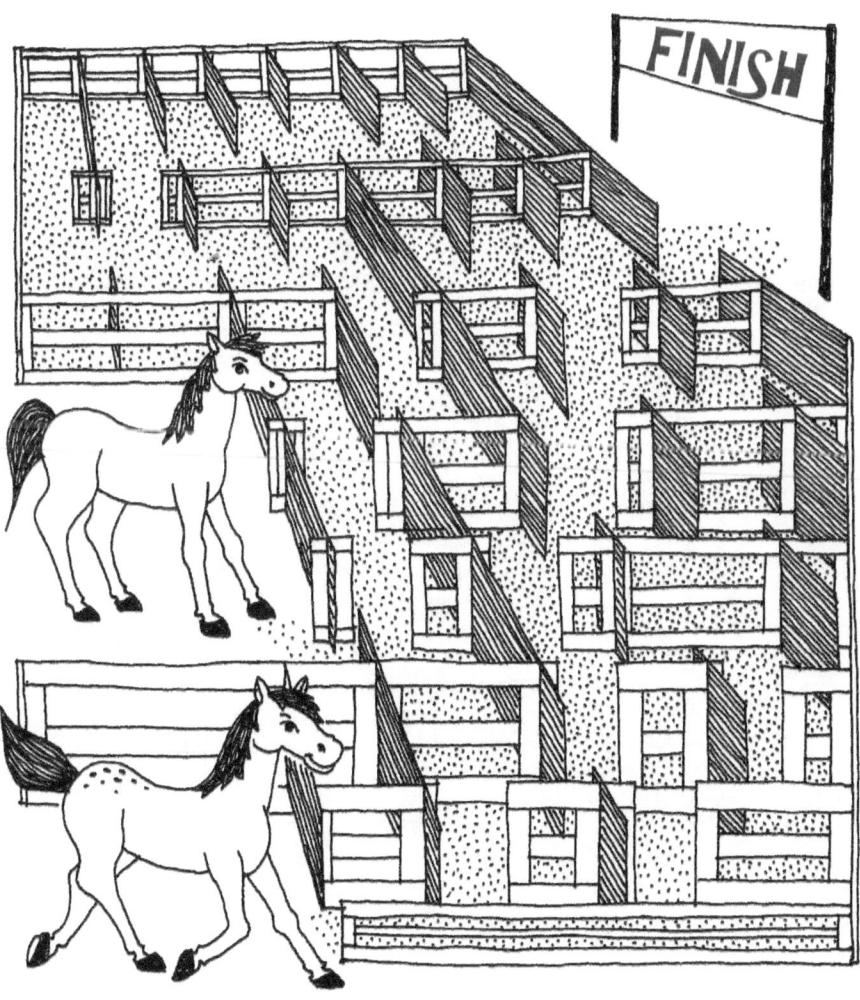

How can the little kitten get out from the house?
You can only follow the arrows, and you can only
touch once the points in crossroads.

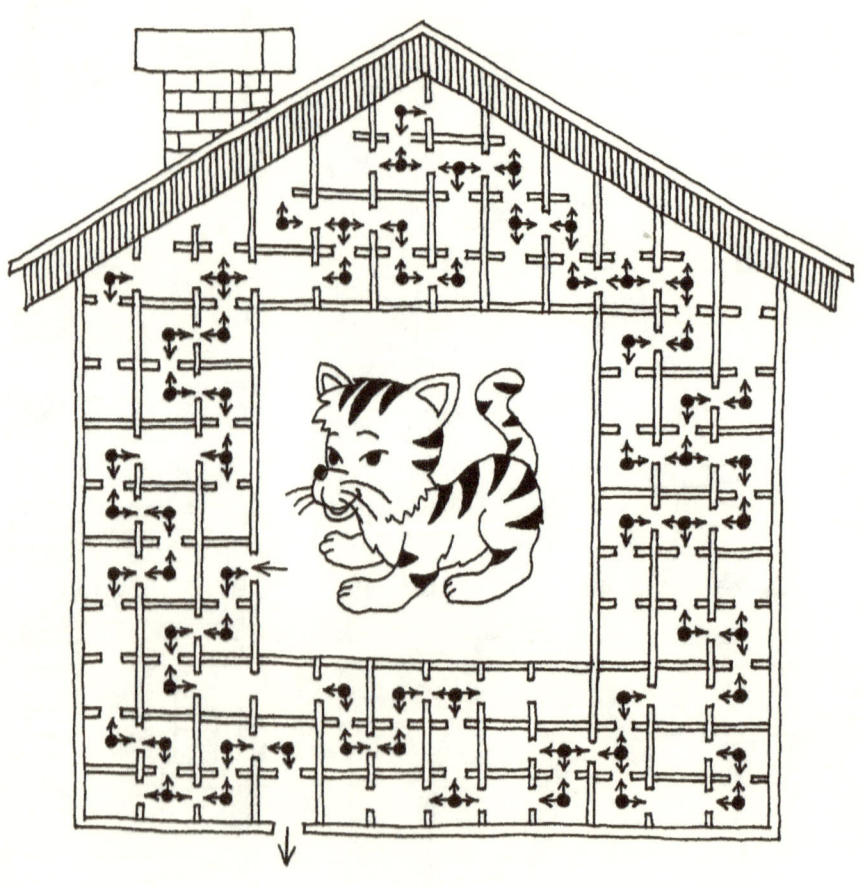

Help Joe to get down the ladders, so
he can find his fallen stick!
On an other way help him to climb up to his sheep.

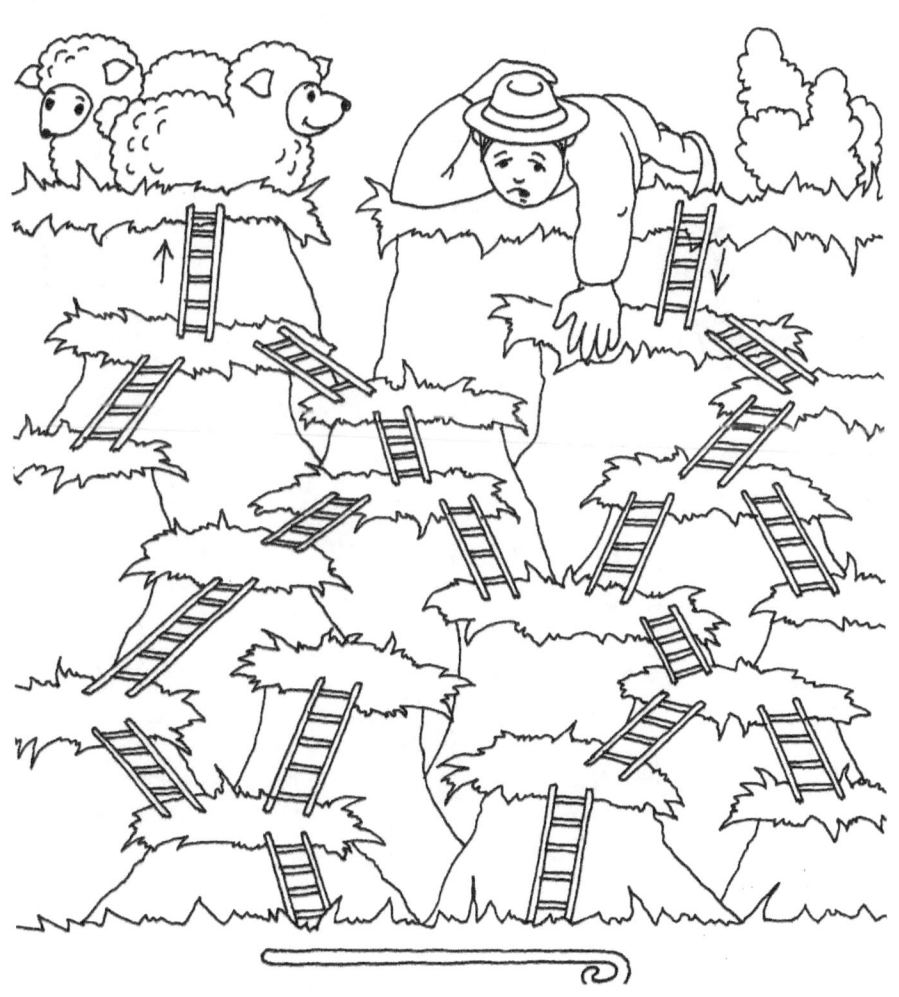

Bird Bobby wants to eat some cherries.
Help him, which way he should use to reach the tree.
You can not fly over the bushes,
Bird Bobby can only hop on the ground. Mark!

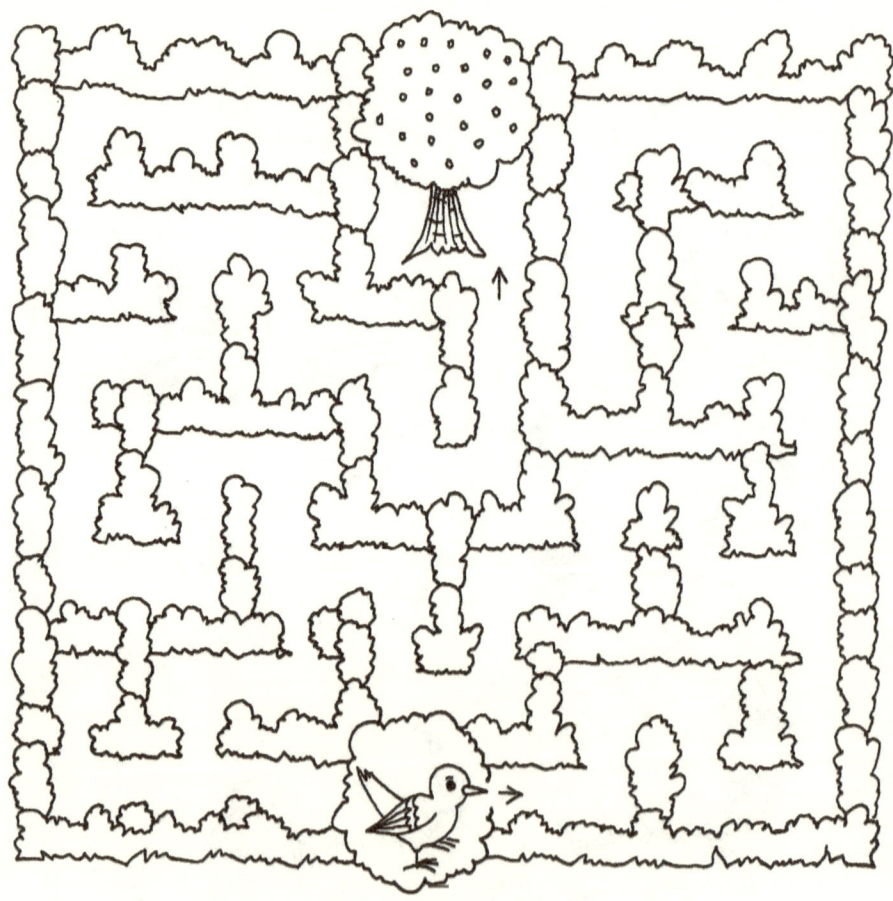

Which way can Mike Mole reach the surface?
Help him!
Mark the right way!

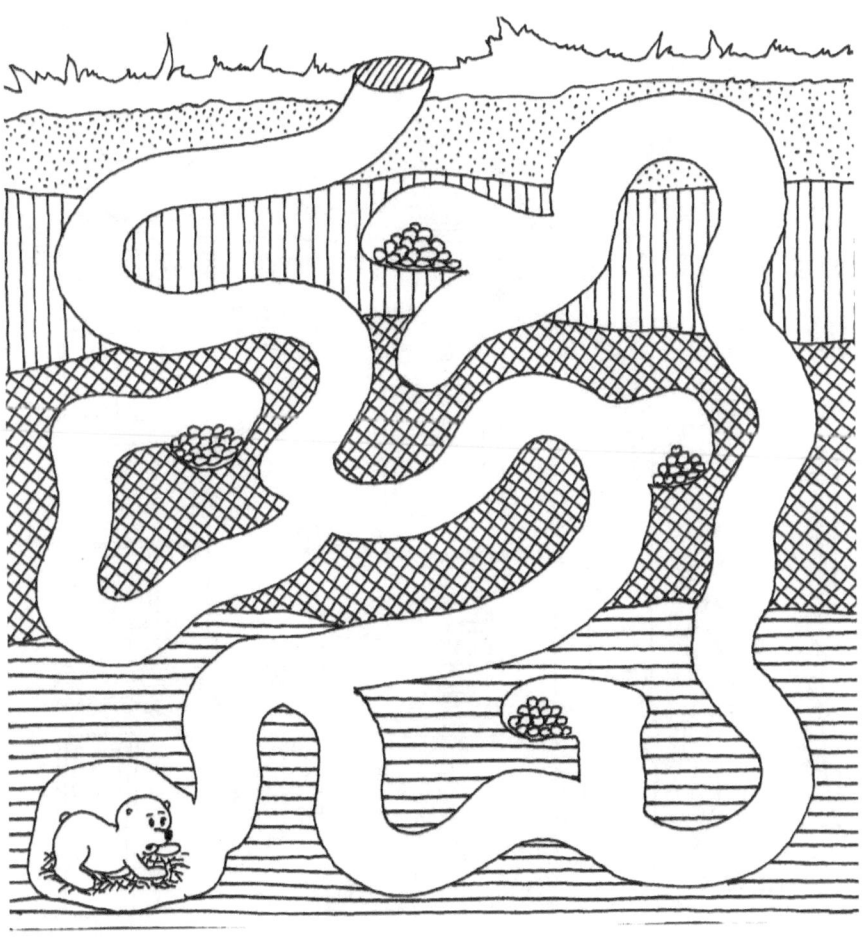

The chimney sweeper can not get off the roof.
Firemen help him. Which way can they bring down
the chimney sweeper?
Mark the way?

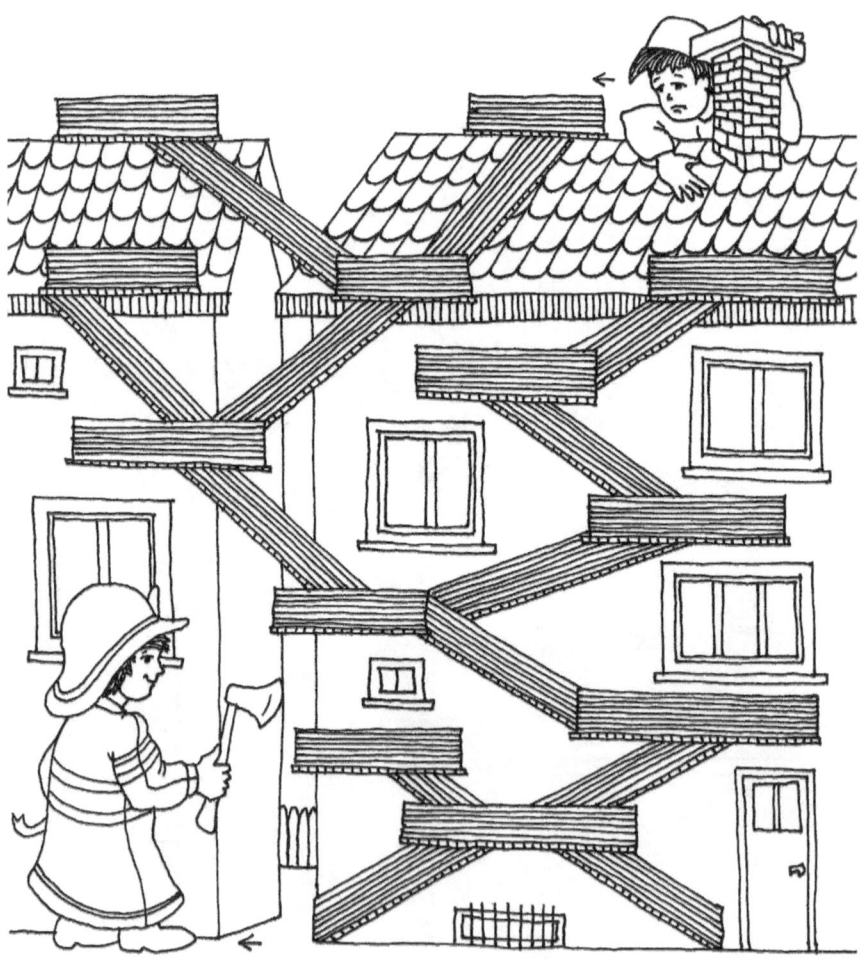

The little chick fell down to the well.
Help her to go up!
The stairs and ladders will help you!
Mark!

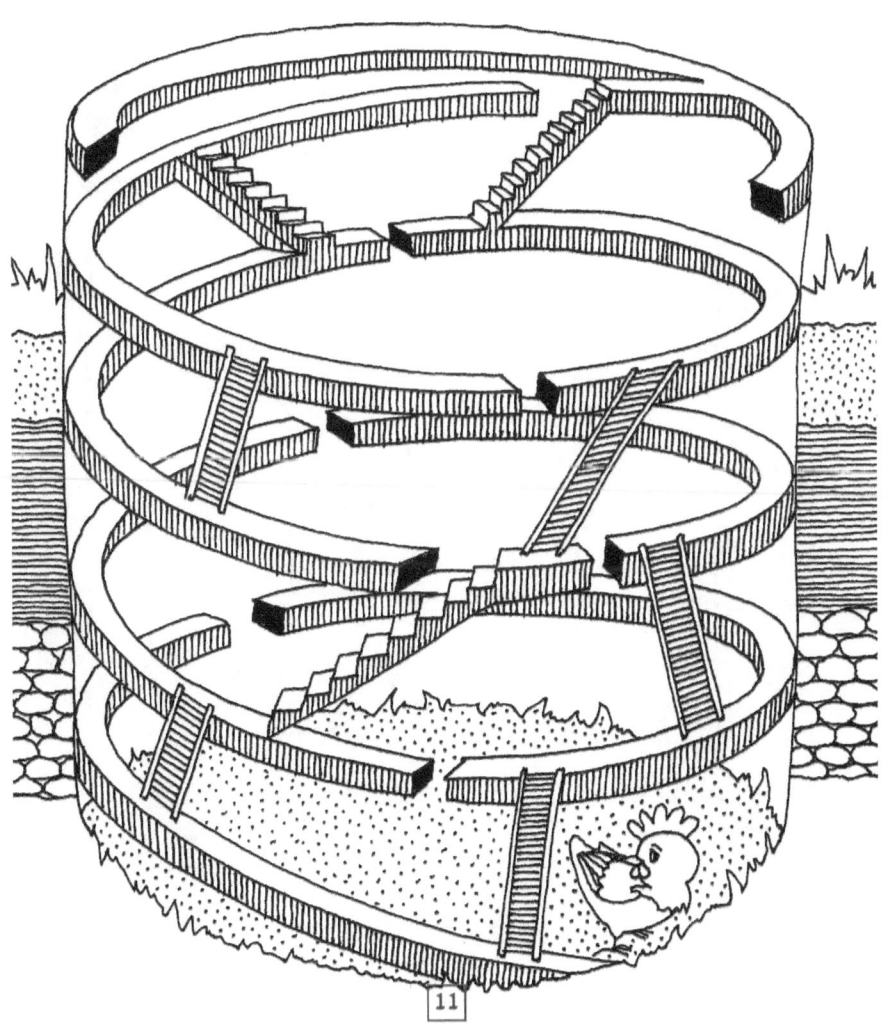

Paul has lost his money.
Help him to find it!
(It is a little bit hard, but I think you can do it!
Come on!)

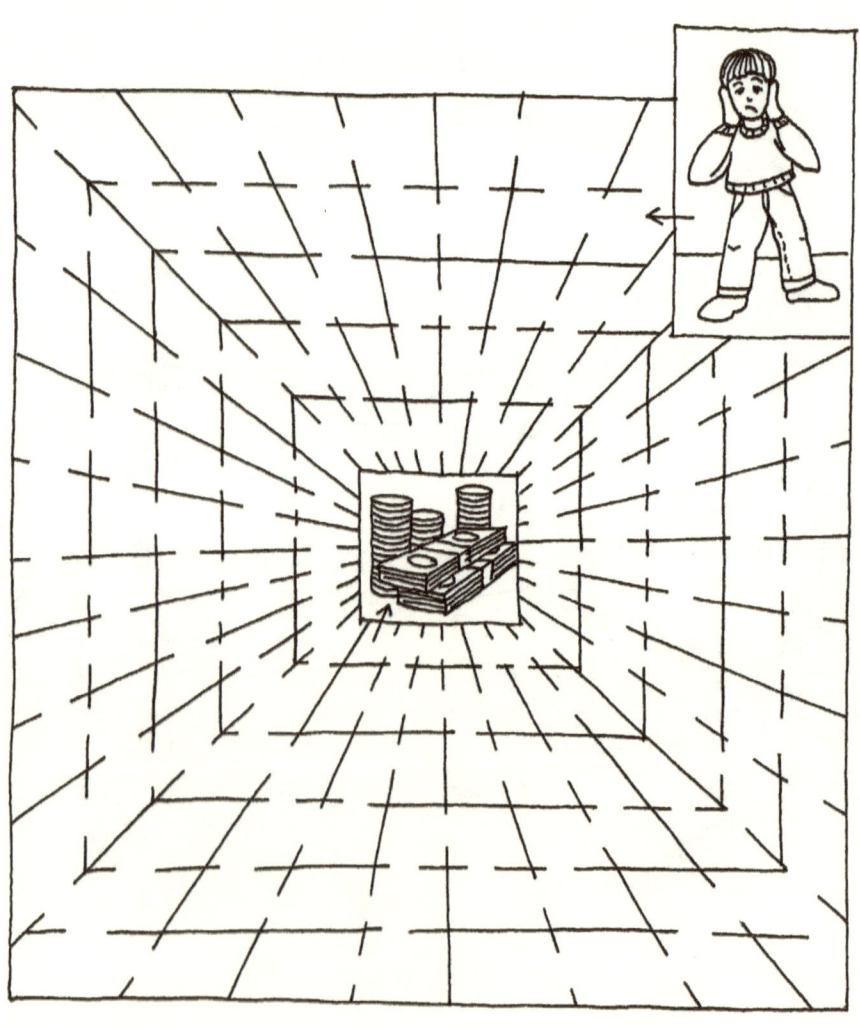

Which bear is coming out from the cave?
Mark!

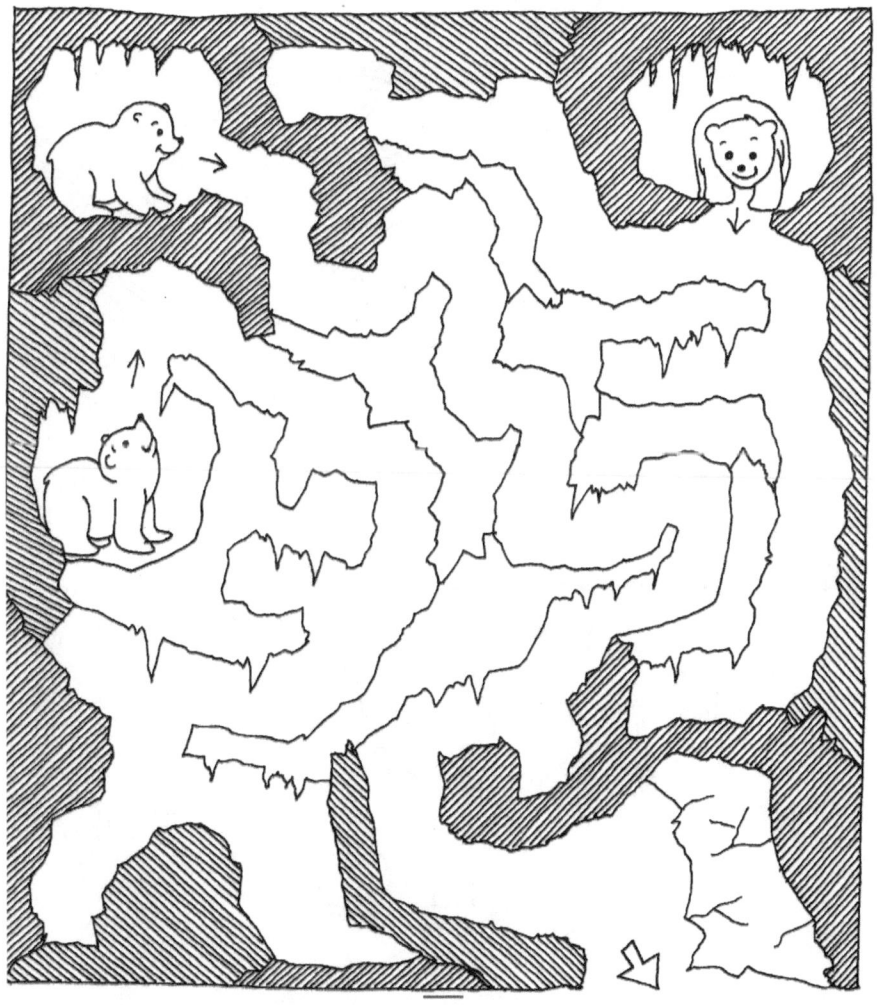

Which key opens the door?
Mark!
(It is a little bit hard, but I think you can do it!
Come on!)

Julie is collecting mushrooms in the forest.
How many mushrooms is she able to find?
Circle the mushrooms that she finds and can collect!

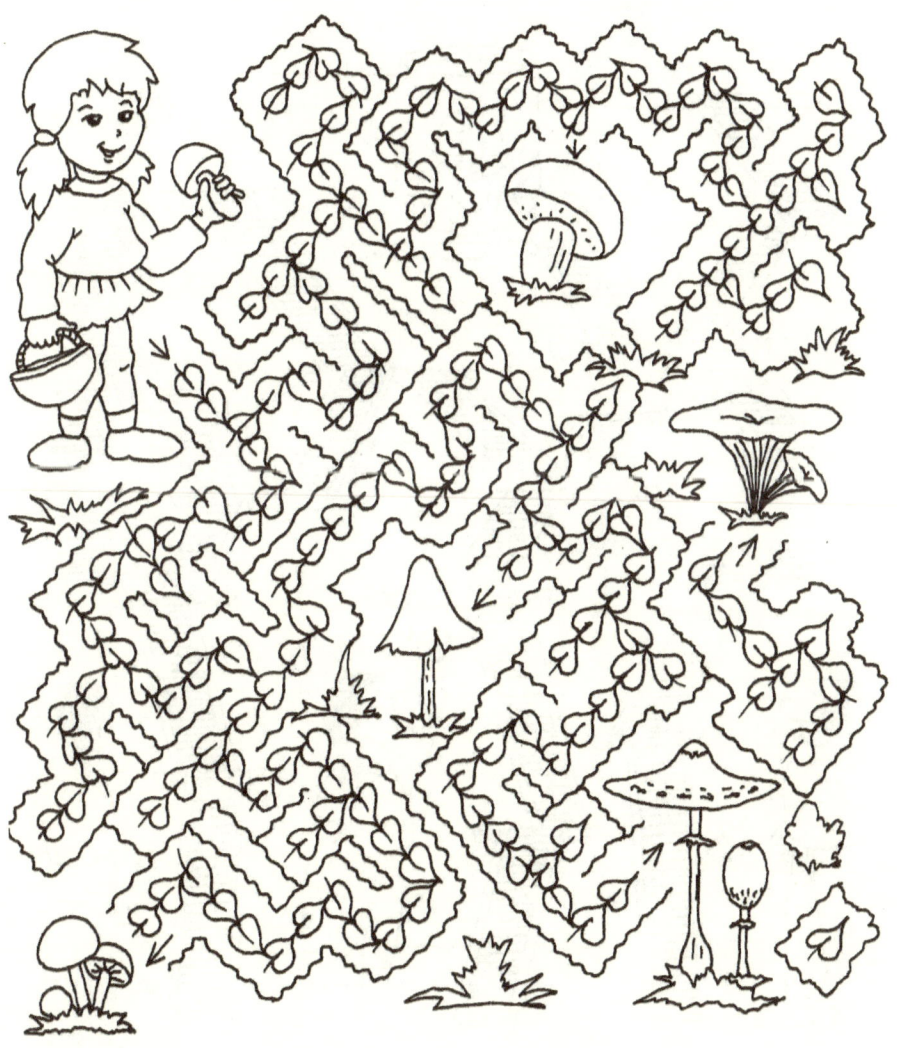

The kitten was hiding in a jug when she stuck.
She can not get out.
Which children can save her? Mark!

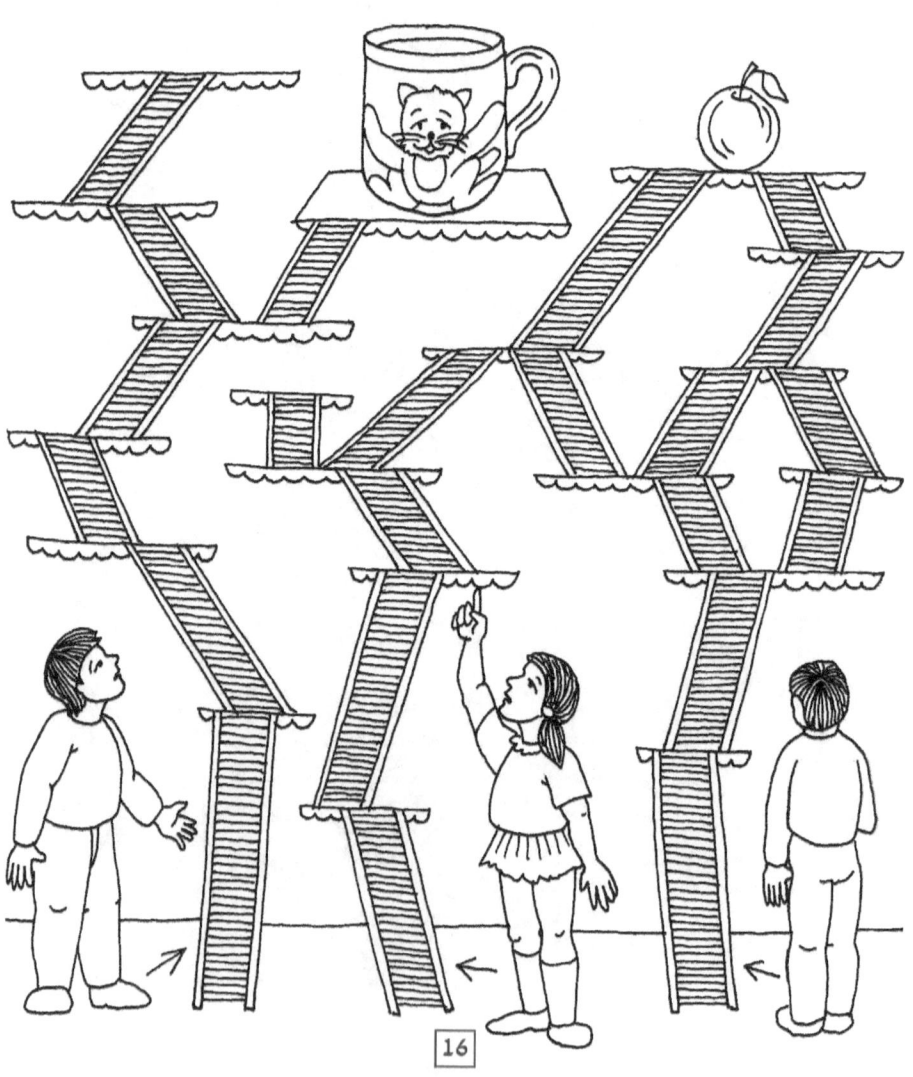

George would like to go up to the third floor.
Help him by marking his way!
(It is a little bit hard, but I think you can do it!
Come on!)

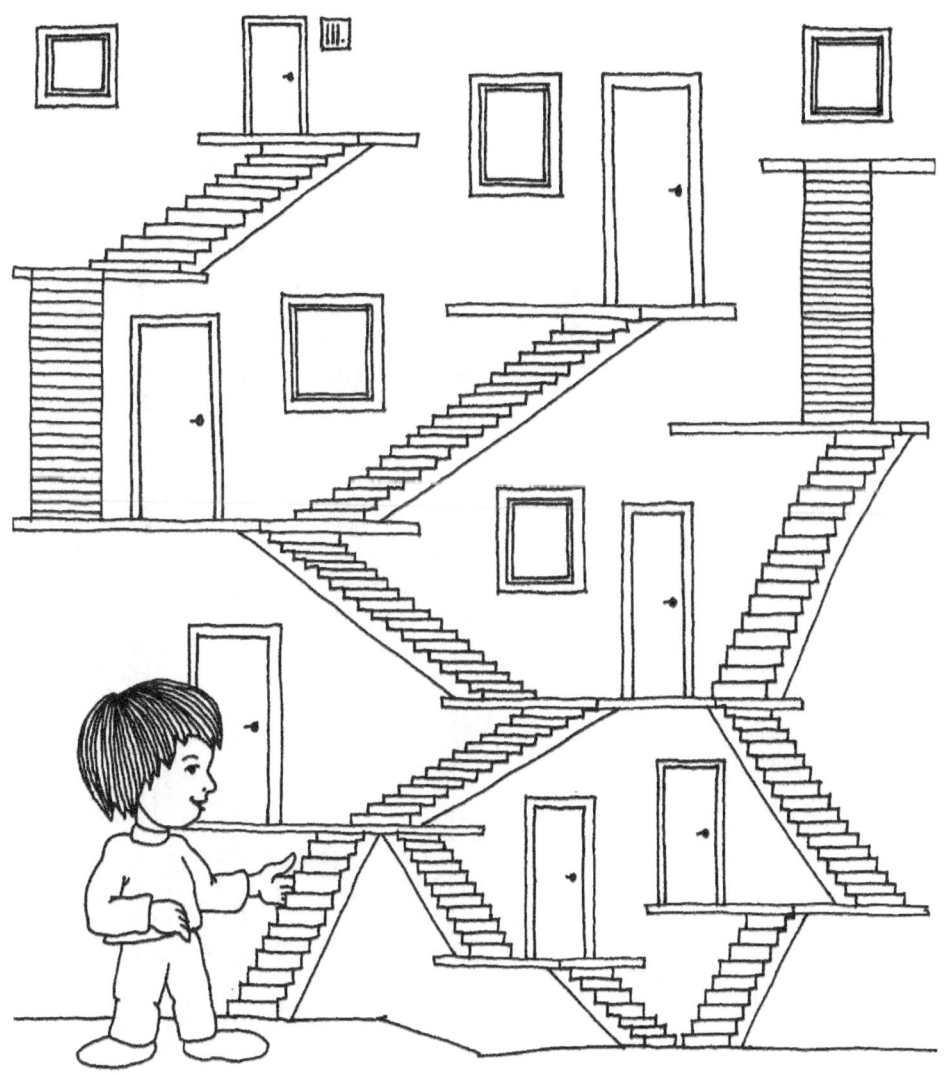

Help Ben to find the full barrel!
(It is a little bit hard, but I think you can do it!
Come on!)

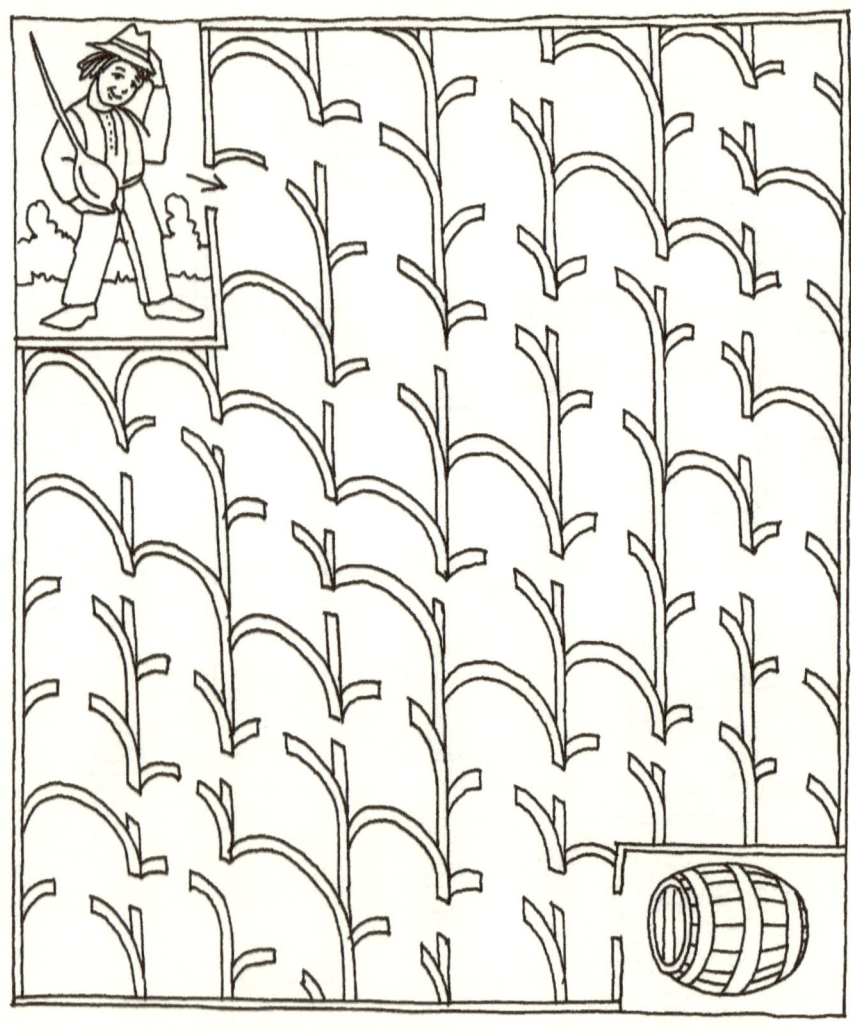

Which kid can reach his father?
Watch the arrows, and mark!
(It is a little bit hard, but I think you can do it!)

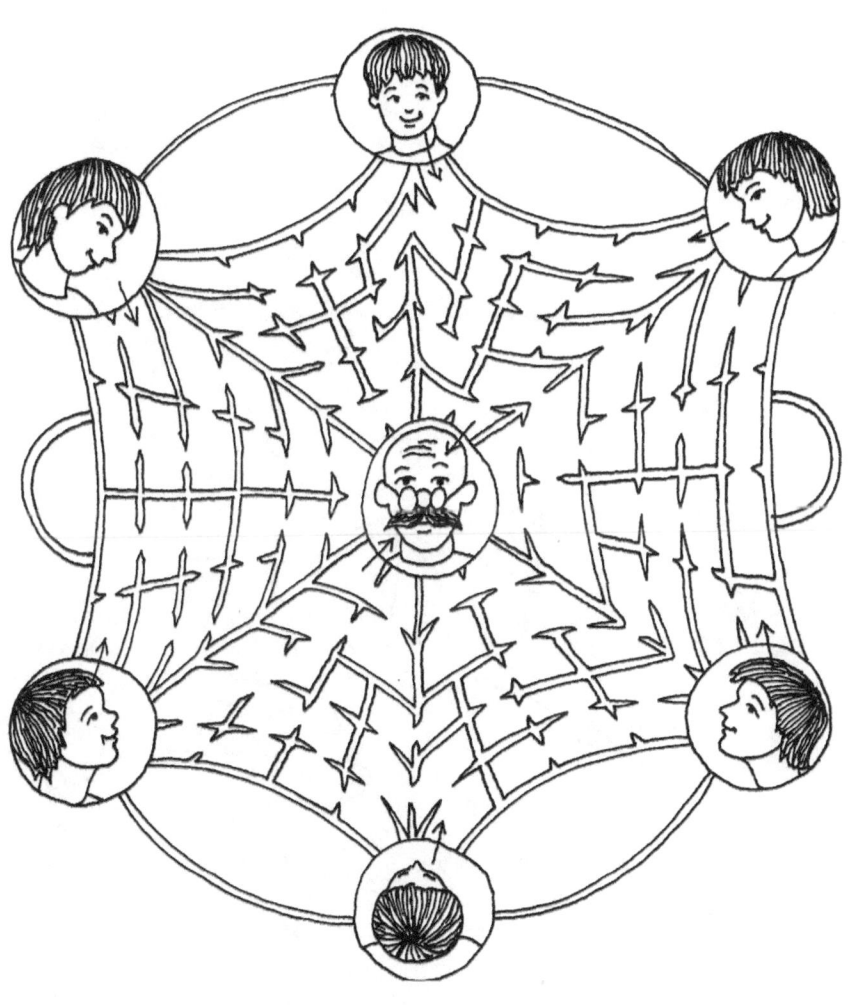

The children are climbing mountain.
Who can get up to the observatory?
Mark!

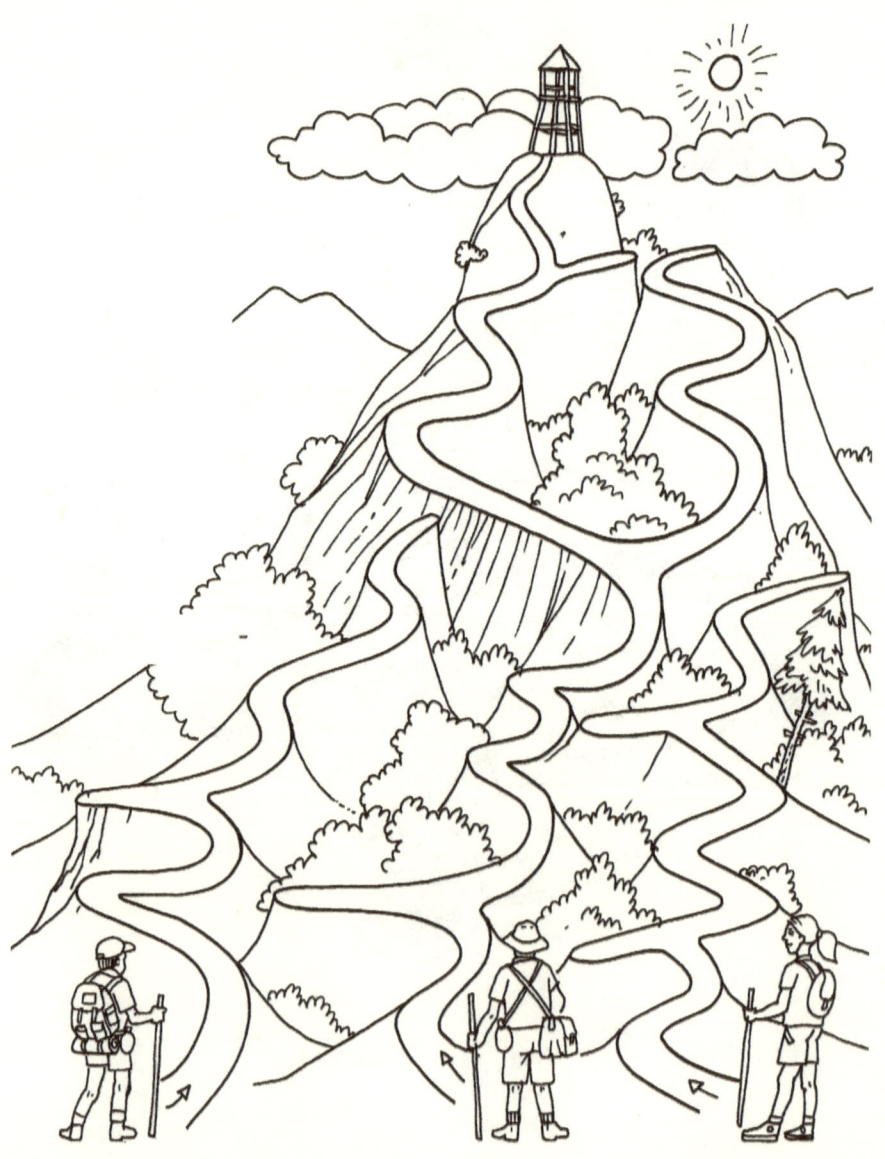

What is going to be my dinner?
Which vegetable can I not reach?
Help to Blair Bunny!
Circle the vegetables that she can eat!

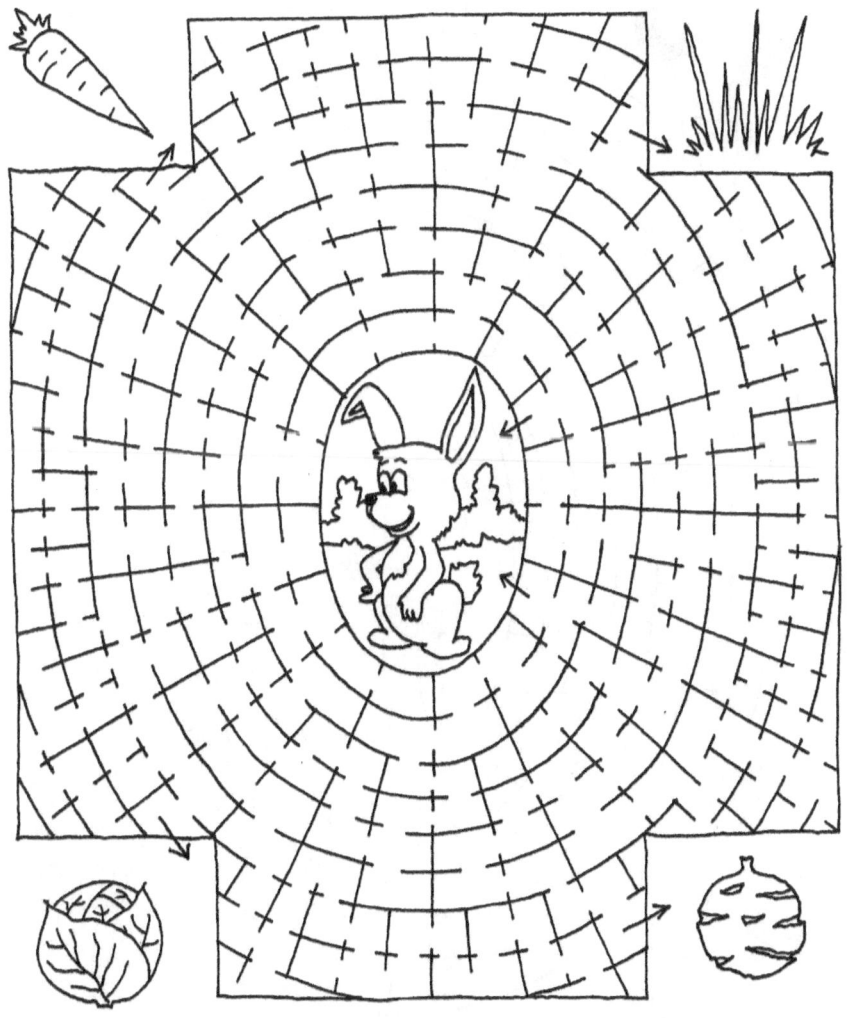

Who is going to be the one that Susan plays with?
Mark the right way!

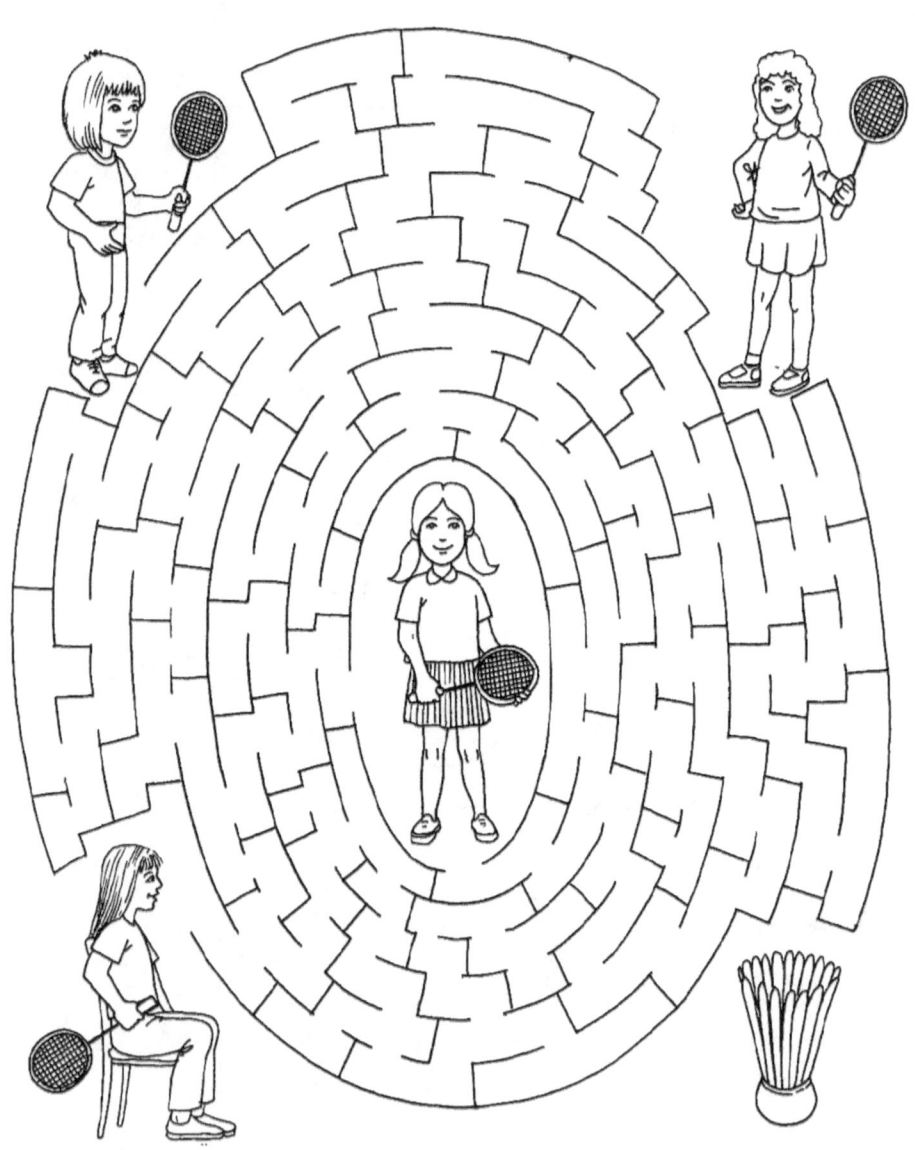

How can the bunny get to the gardener?
Mark!

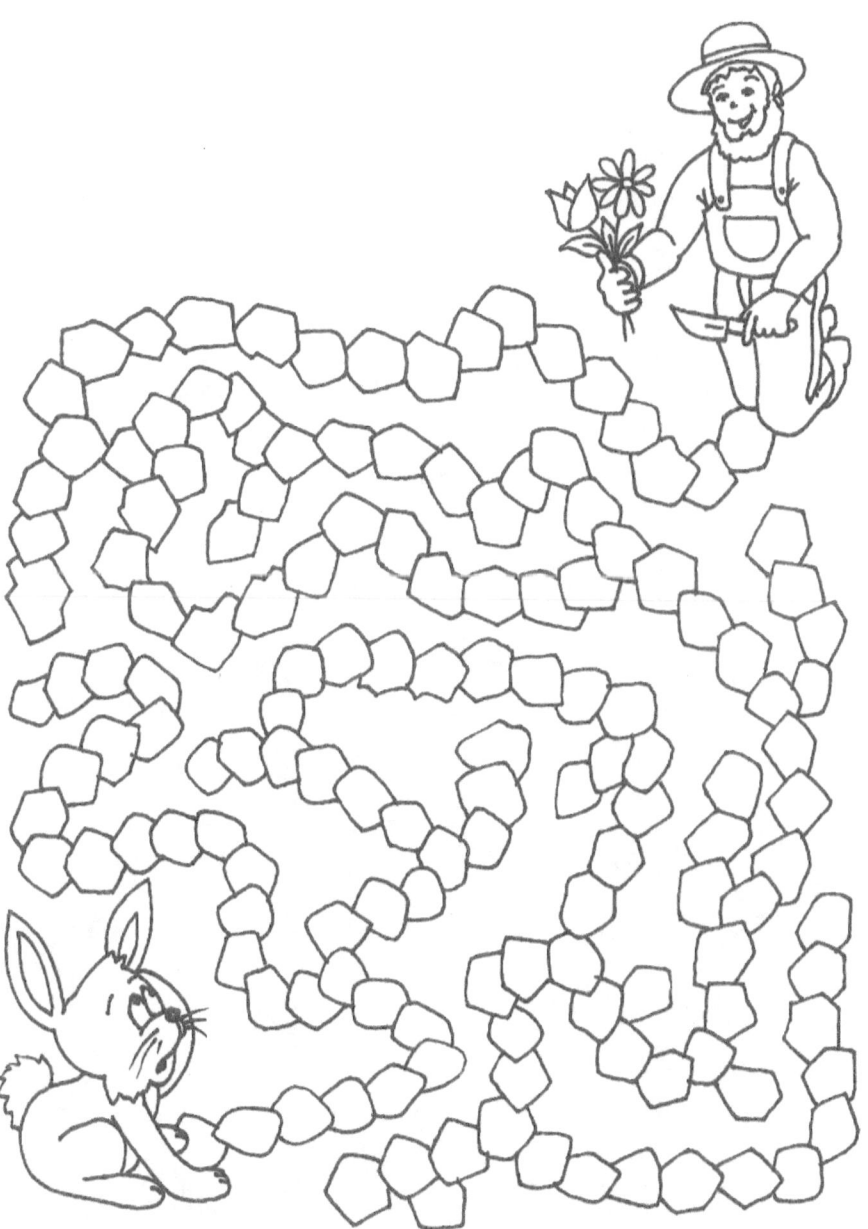

Sam climbed up to the roof, and he can not go down.
Firemen help him.
Which way should they use to bring Sam down?

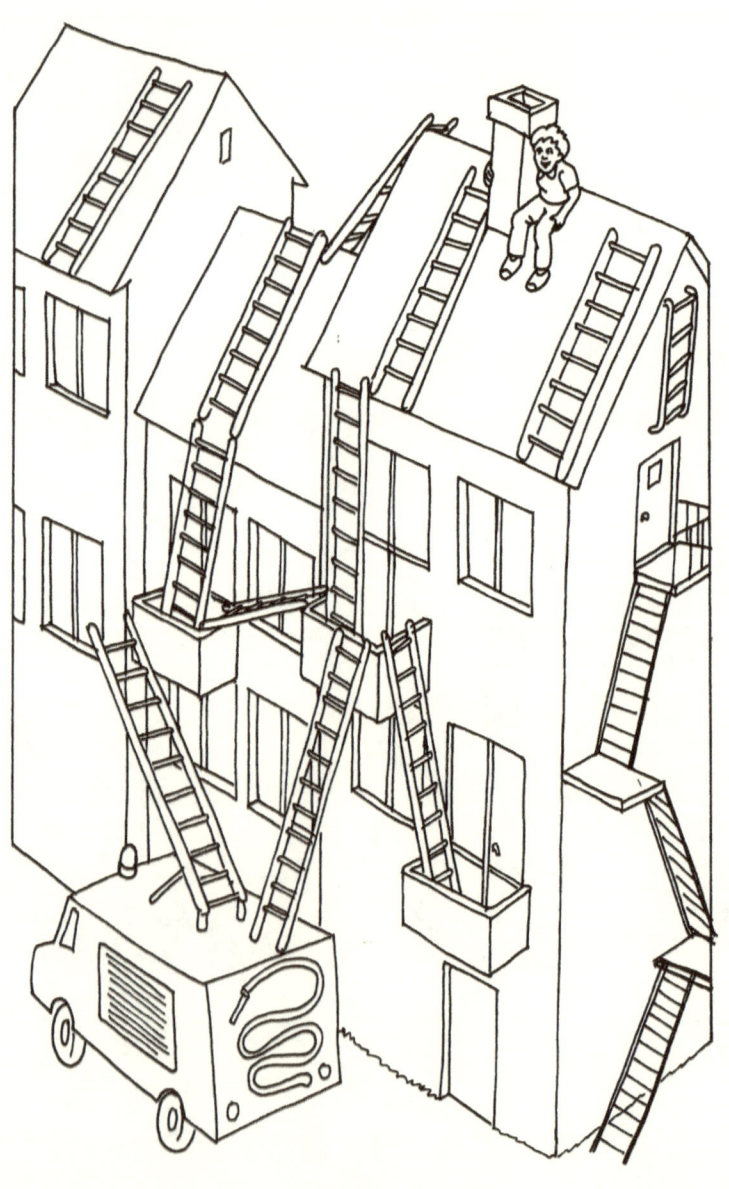

Penny, Pete and Phil are climbing mountain.
Who can reach the top?
(It is a little bit hard, but I think you can do it!
Come on!)

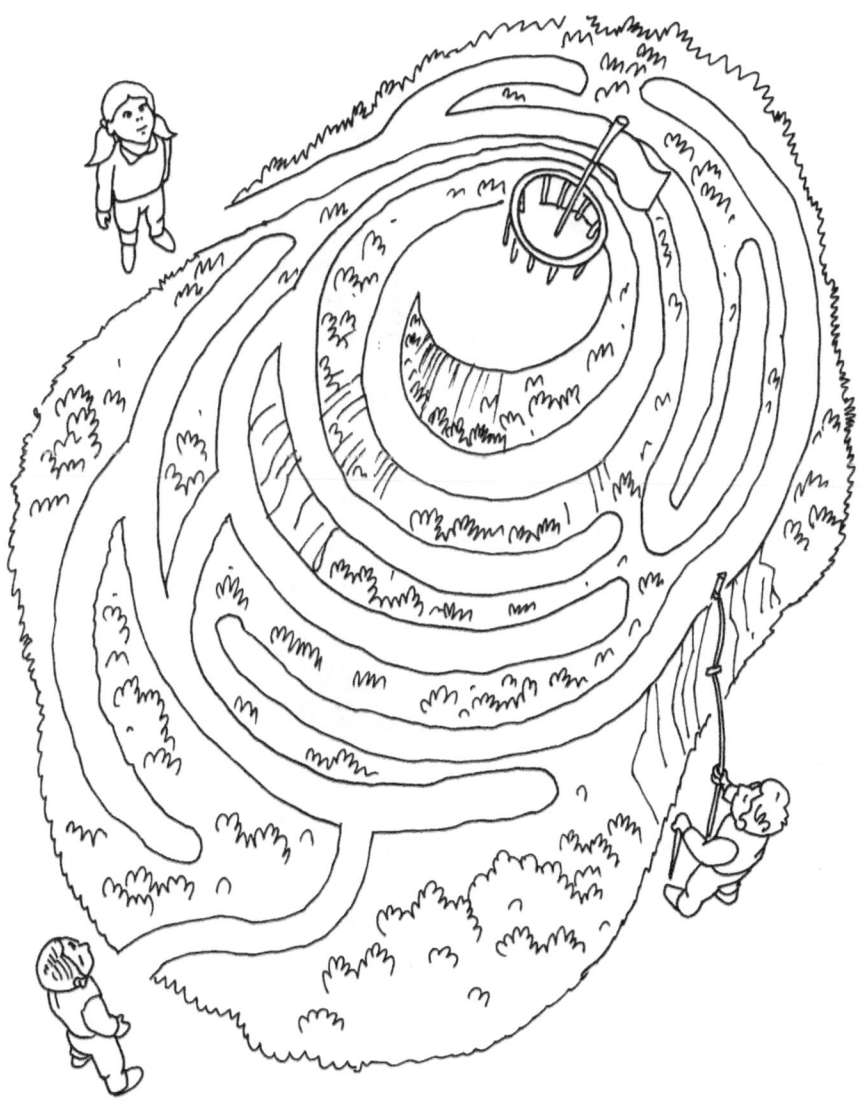

Lead the bee worker to his Queen! Mark!
(It is a little bit hard, but I think you can do it!
Come on!)

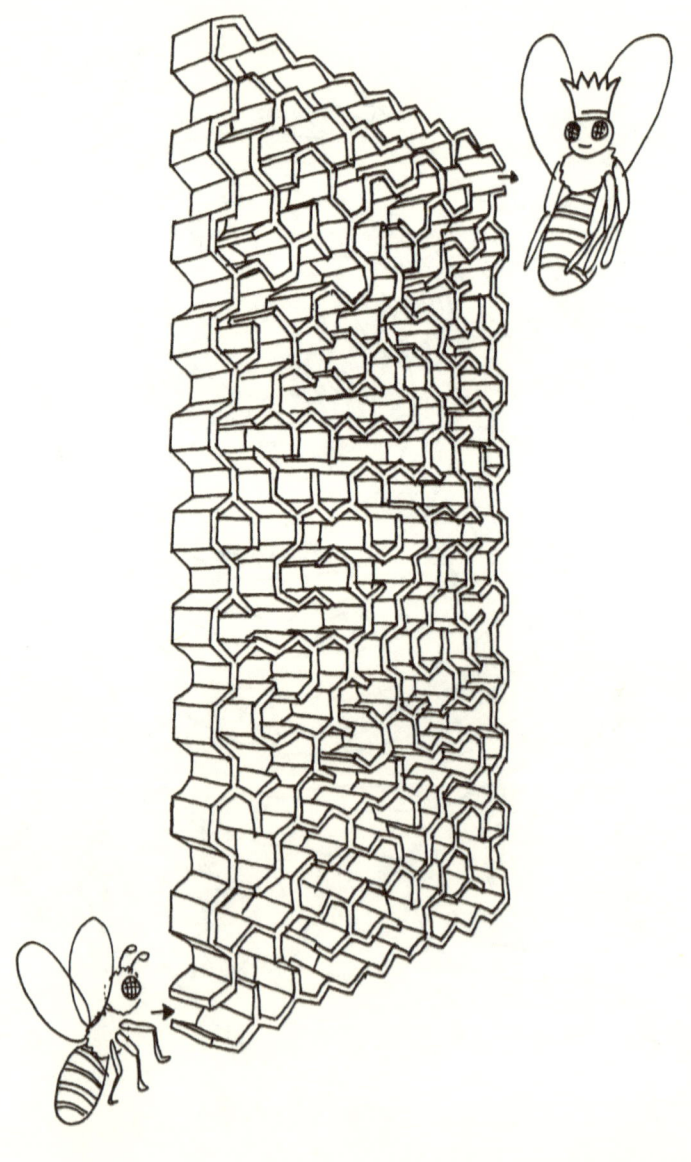

Which horse can get into the barn? Mark!
(It is a little bit hard, but I think you can do it!
Come on!)

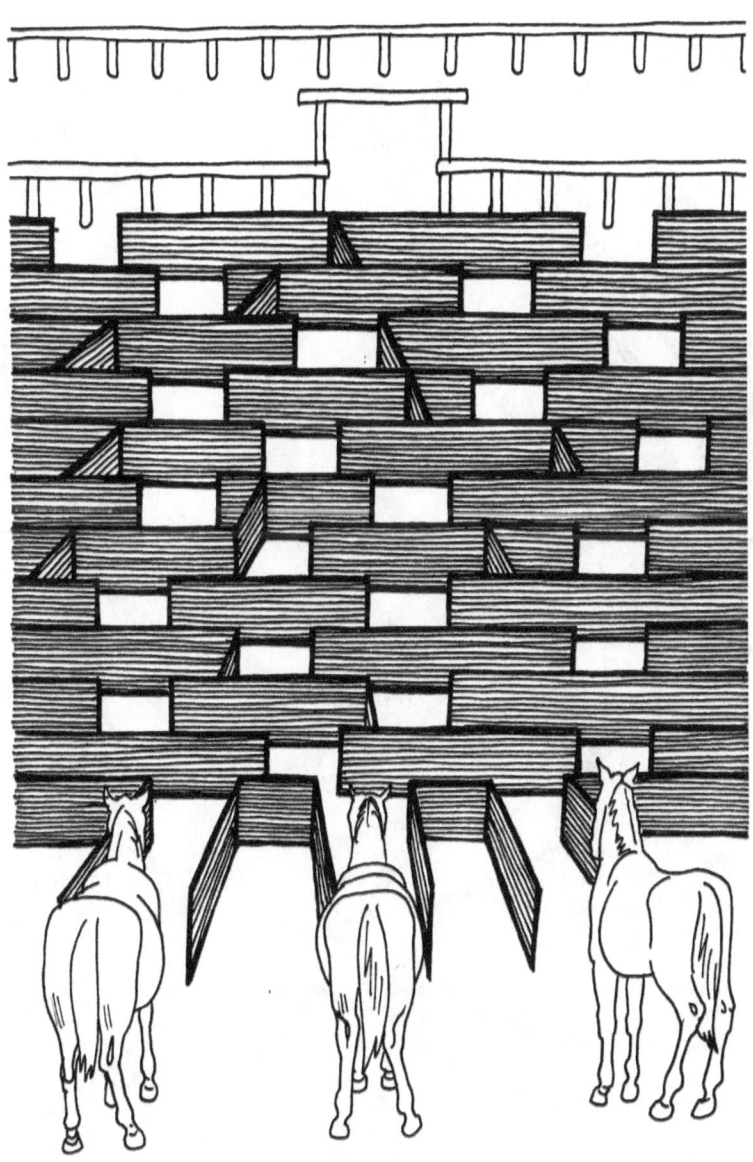

James got lost in the bushes.
Help him to find the right way out!
Mark!

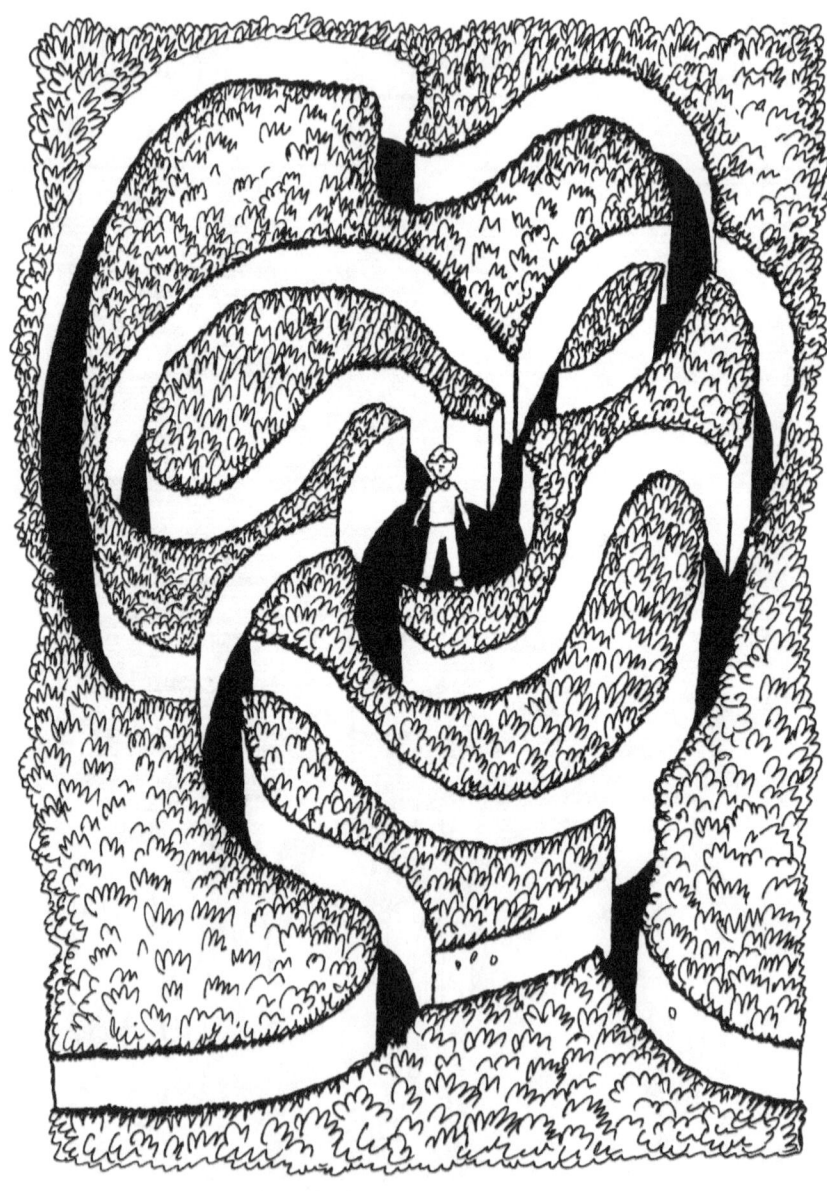

The blond prince has left his white horse.
Help him to find his mount!
Mark!

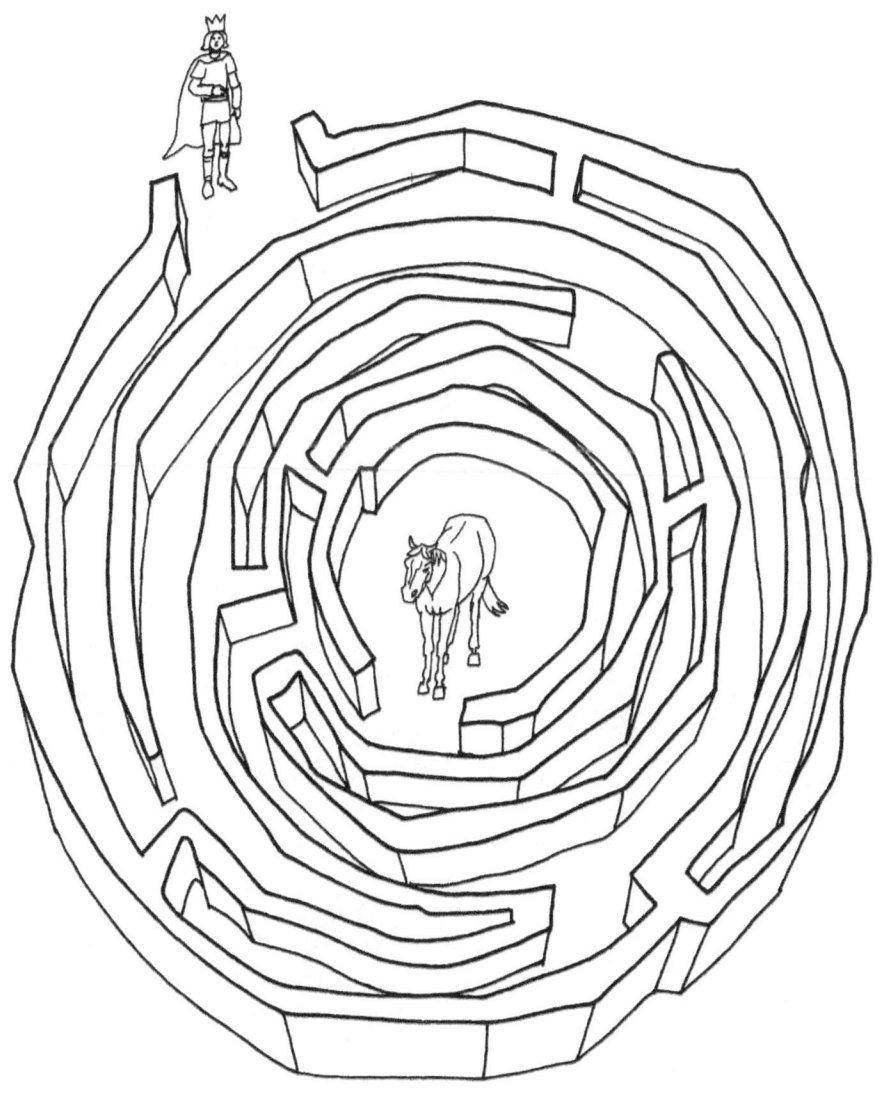

The children are climbing mountain.
Who can get up to the observatory?
Mark!

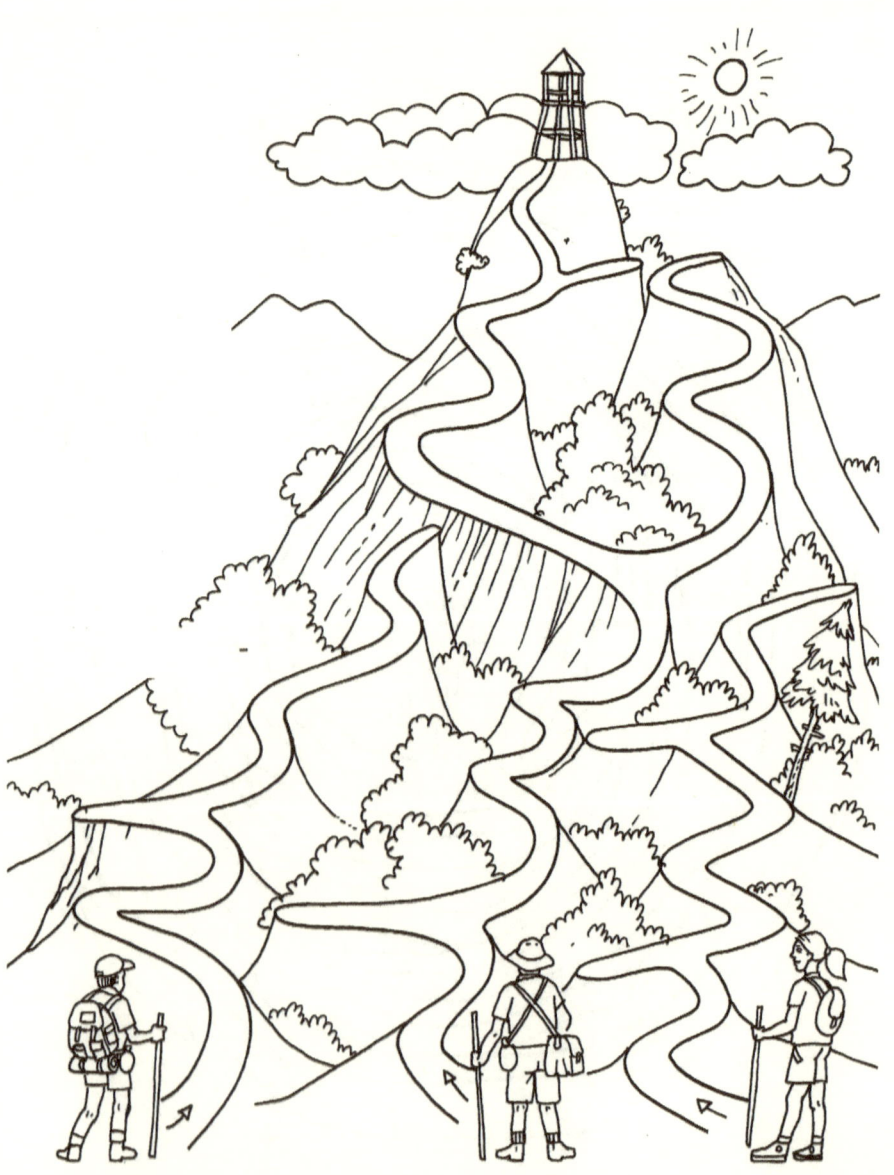

What is going to be my dinner?
Which vegetable can I not reach?
Help to Blair Bunny!
Circle the vegetables that she can eat!

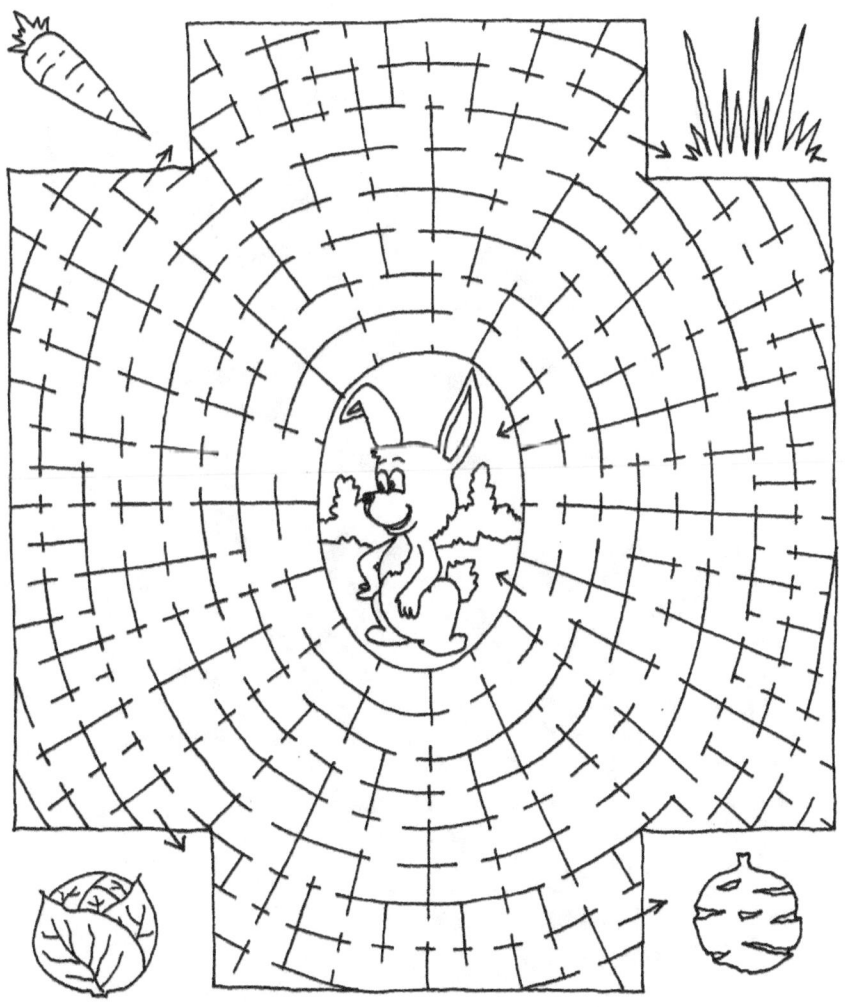

Harry Hedgehog wants to visit his friend.
Help him to get to his friend's house!
Mark!

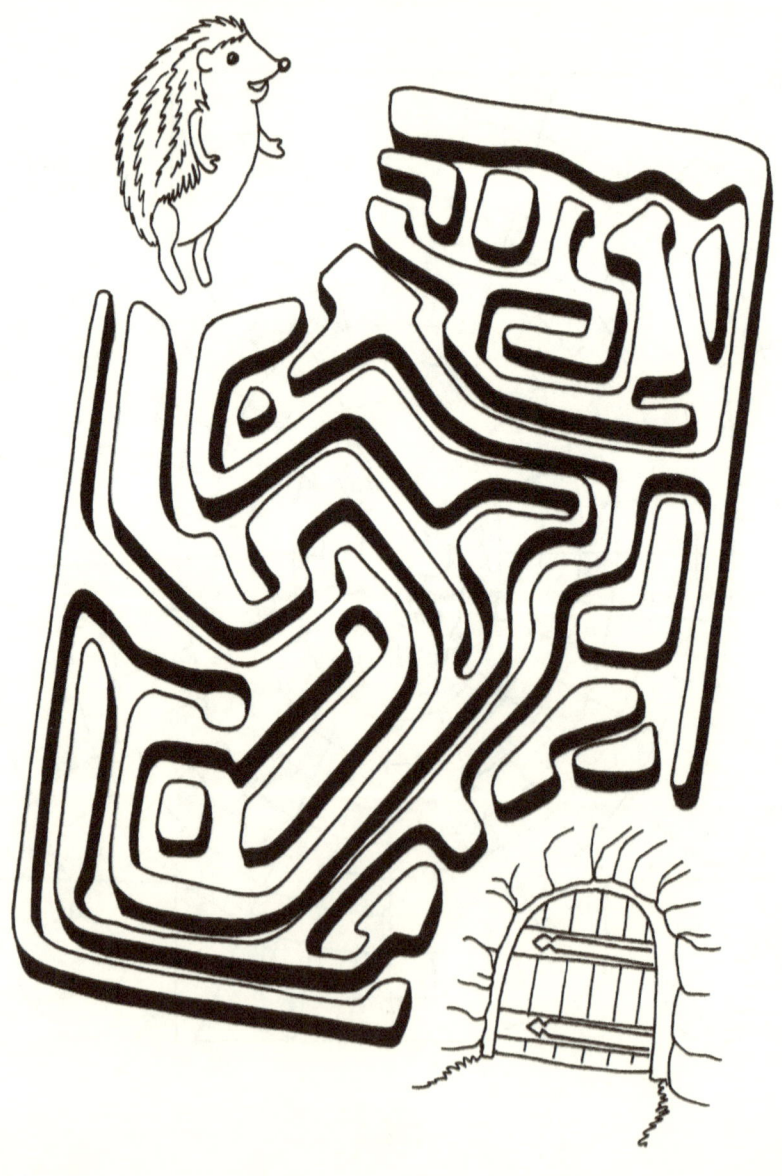

The treasure of a pharaoh has been
hidden in the pyramid.
Help the archeologist to find it!
Mark!

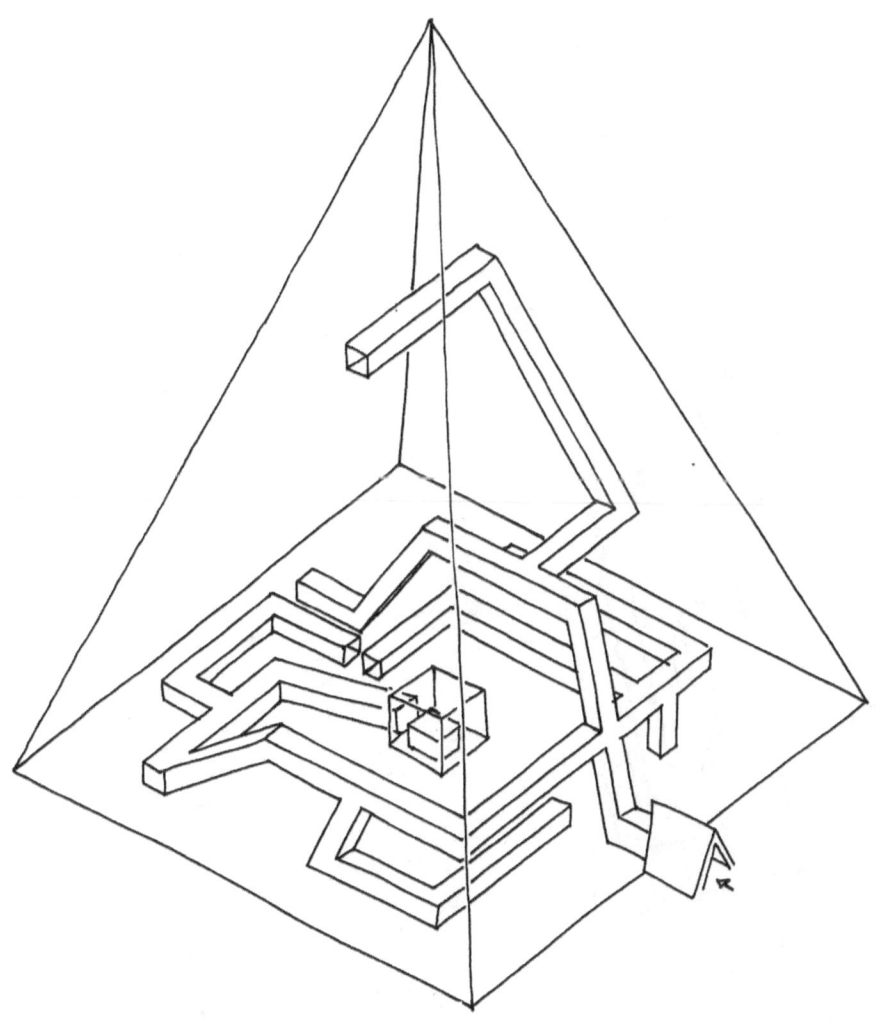

Fred Frog has lost.
Help him to get out from the labyrinth.
Mark!

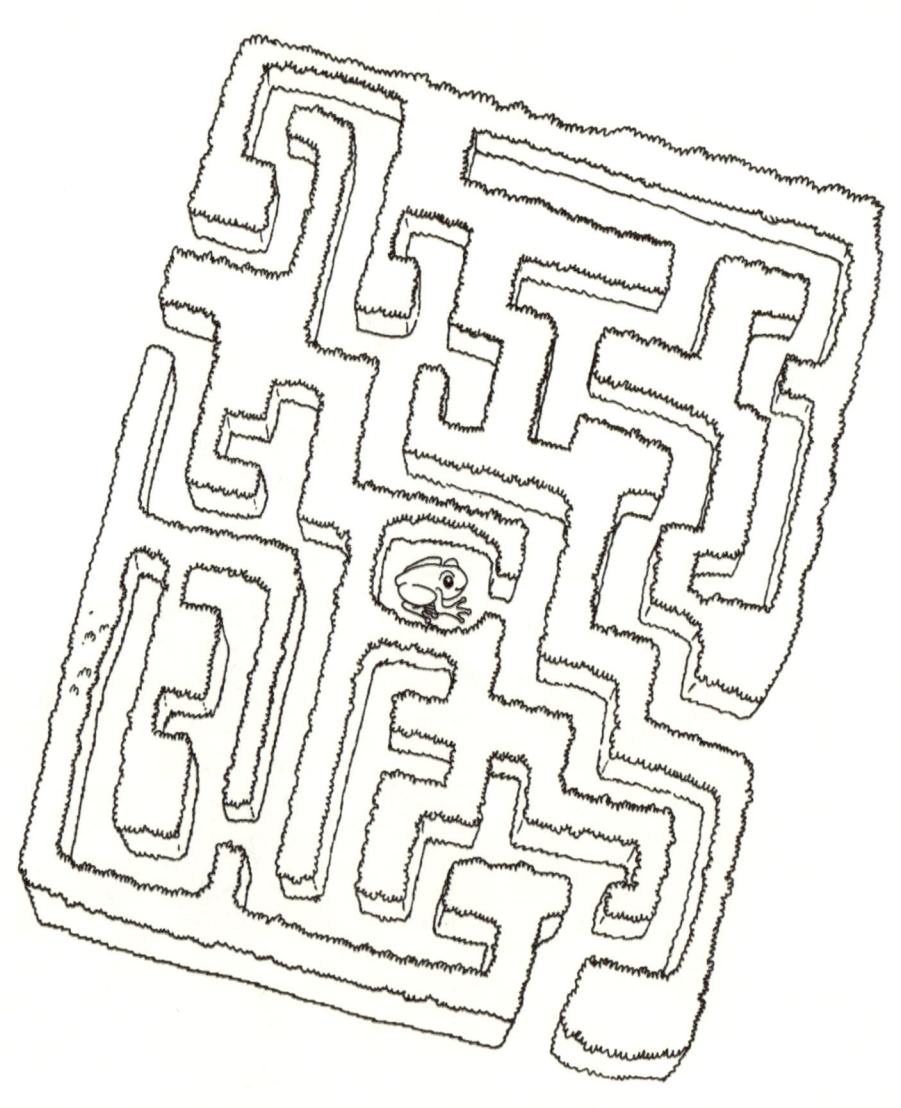

Bart Bear would like to eat some honey.
Help him to climb up the top of his honey jar!
Mark!

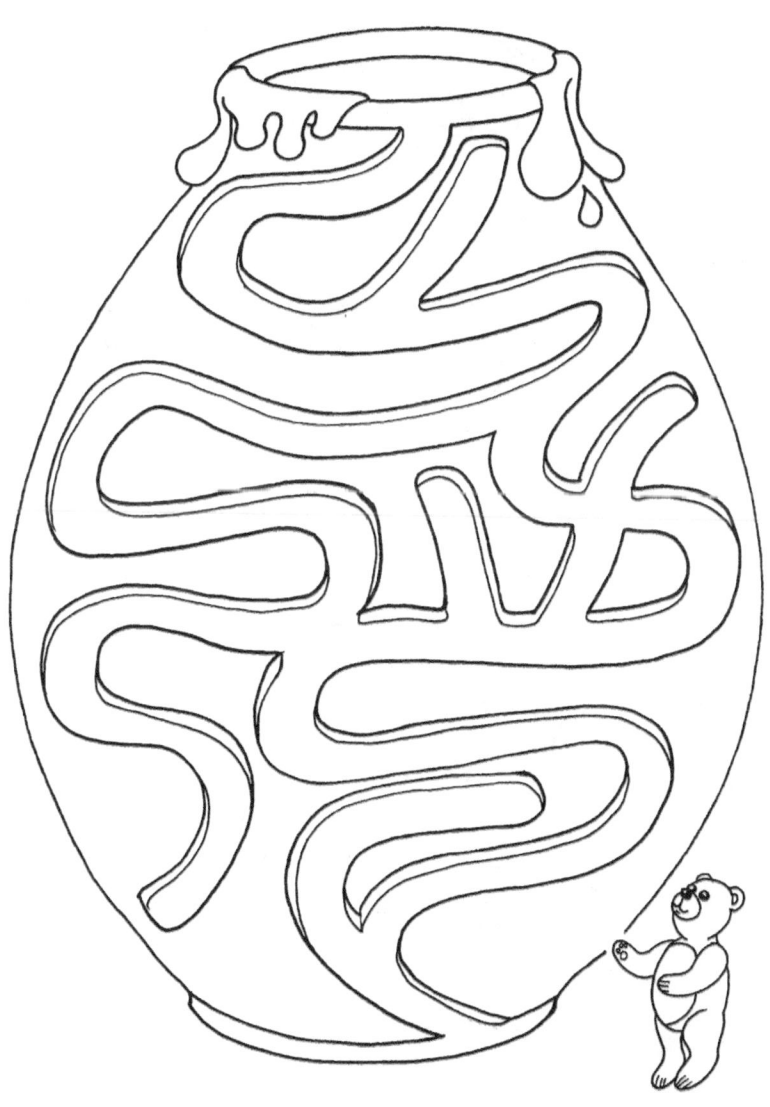

There are amazing treasures in the magical castle.
Who can find the treasure first?
Mark!

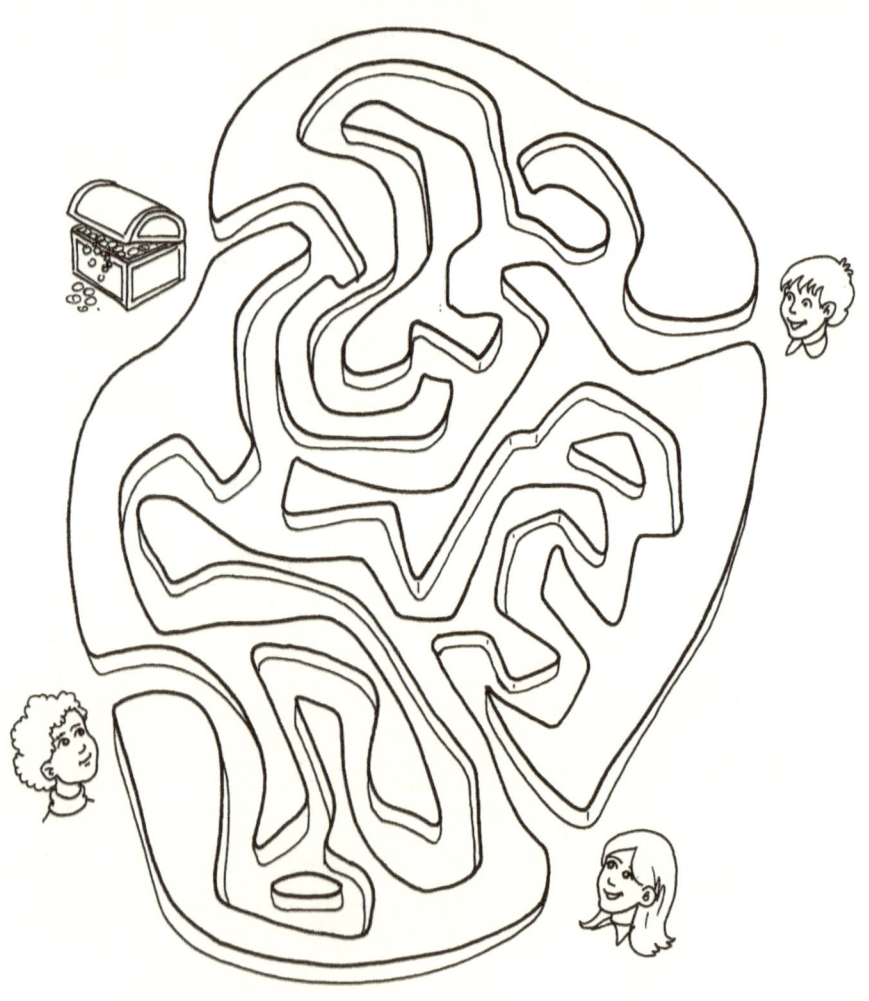

Gary Goose has lost.
Help him to find his Mom!
Mark his way!

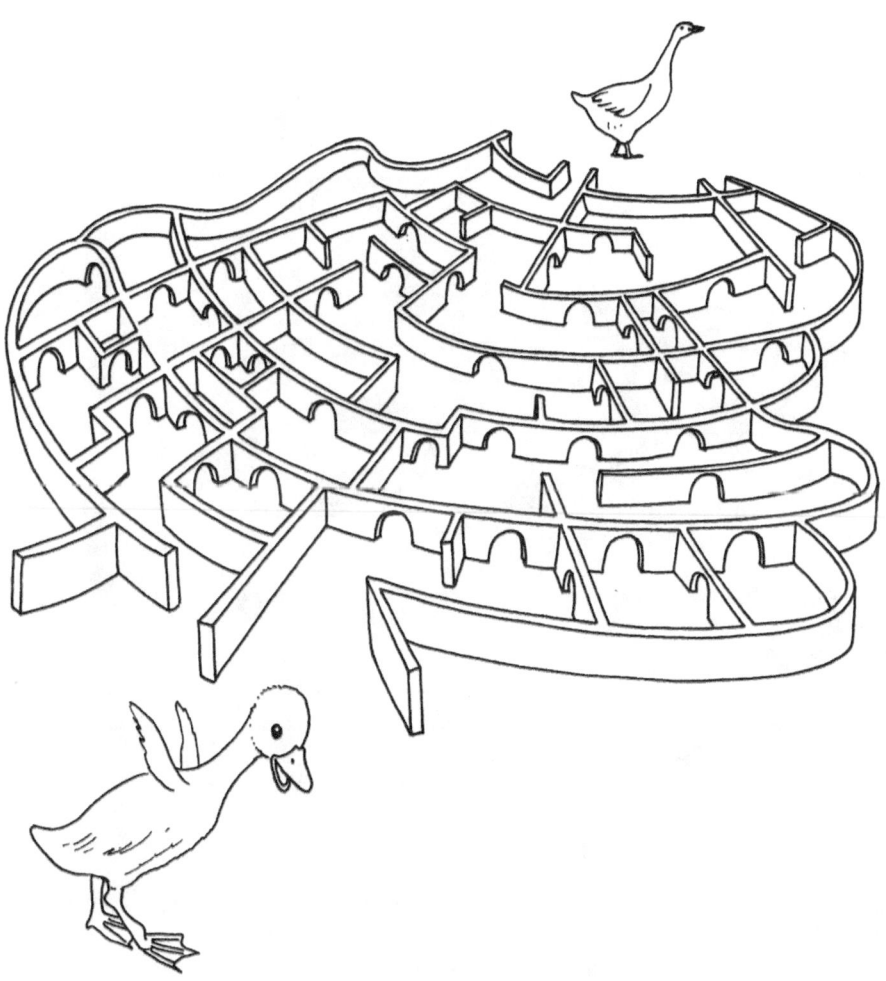

The little mouse is very hungry!
He would like to eat the cheese.
Help him to find his dinner!
Mark your way!

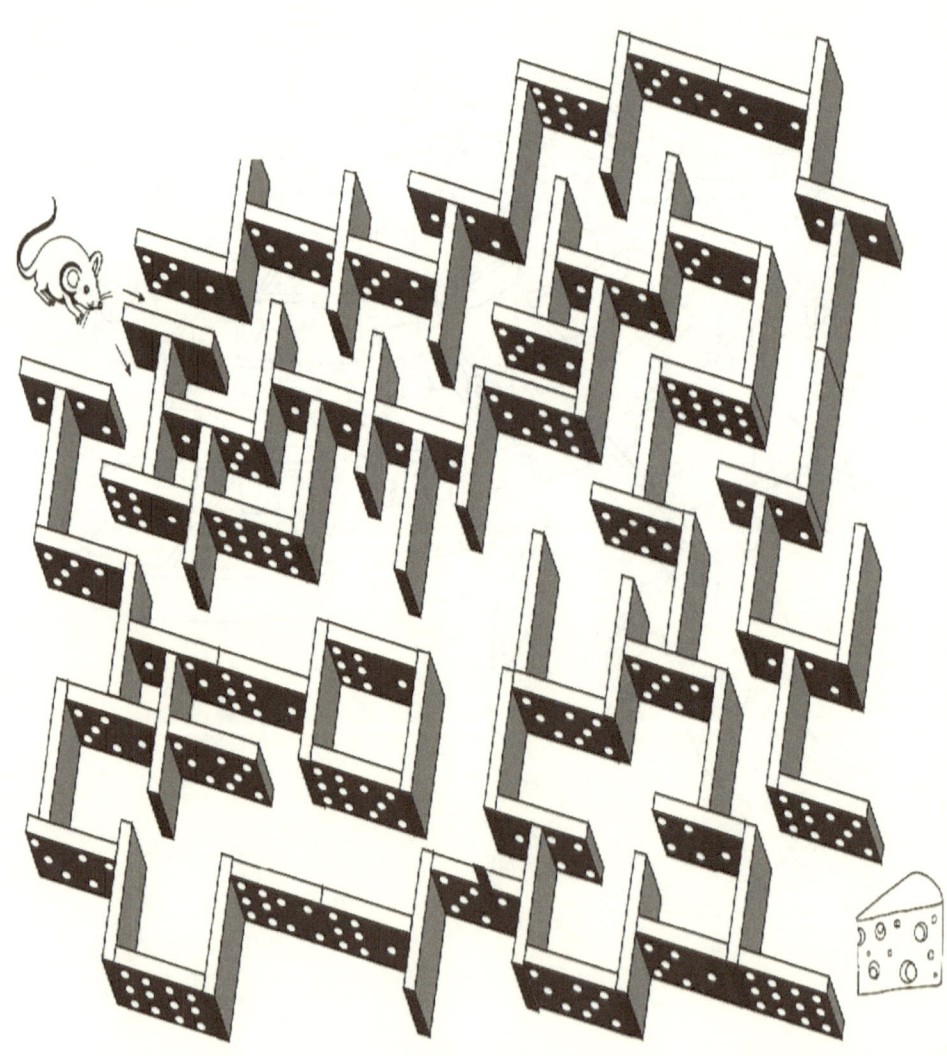

In which order Joe gets to the gifts?
Mark!

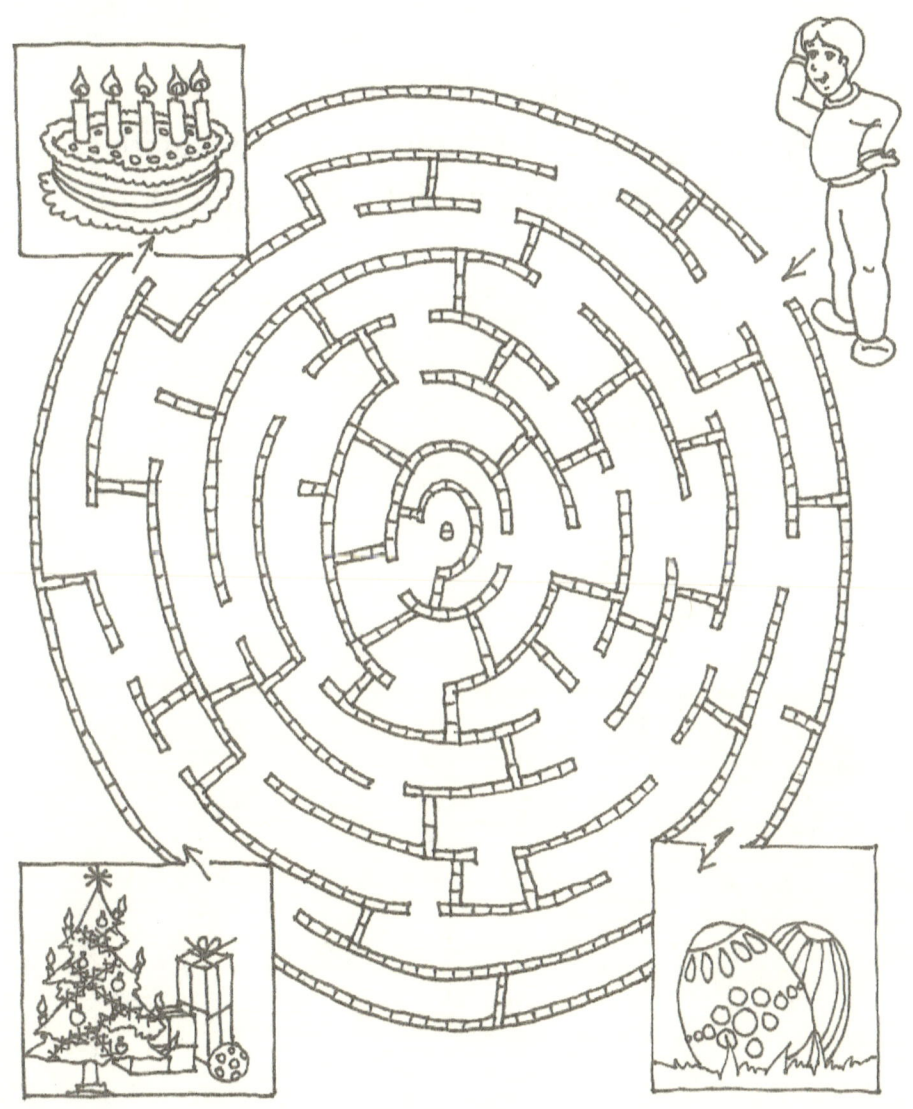

A rich man built a palace with three
swimming pools. One has warm water, one has cold water
and the third is empty. His friend is asking him why?
-You know, there are days when it feels good to swim in a war
watered pool, and on the hot days the cold water feels better.
-But, why do you have the empty pool as well?
-There are days, when I do not feel like swimming.

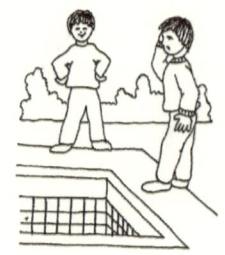

Are the kids arguing?
Who is going to be the who she plays with?
Mark the correct route with different colors!

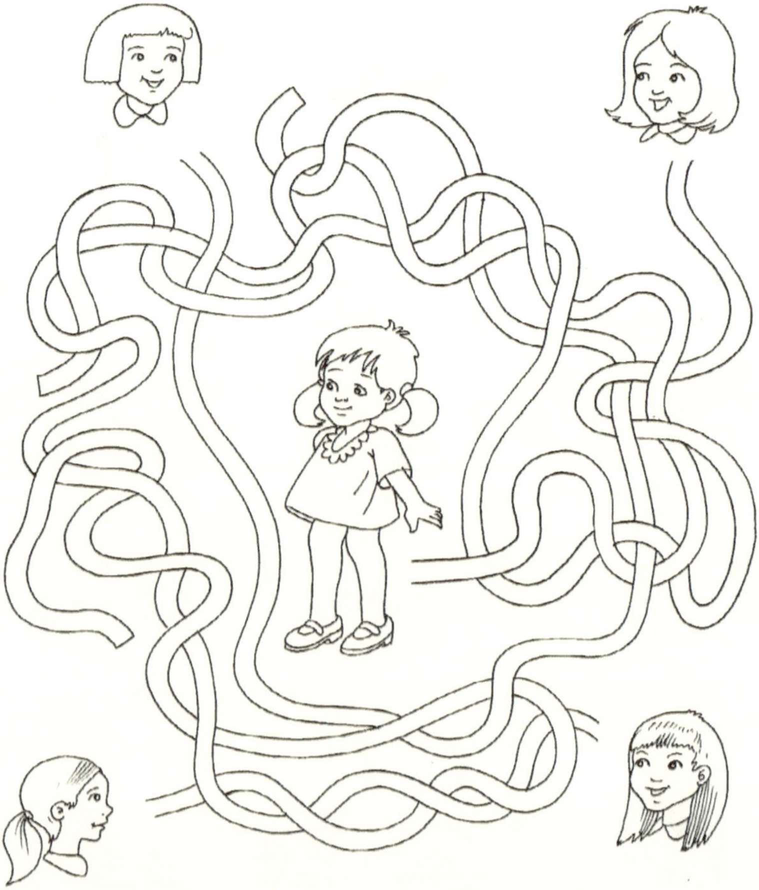

Help to Robby Rat to get to the surface via the water supplying system's pipes.

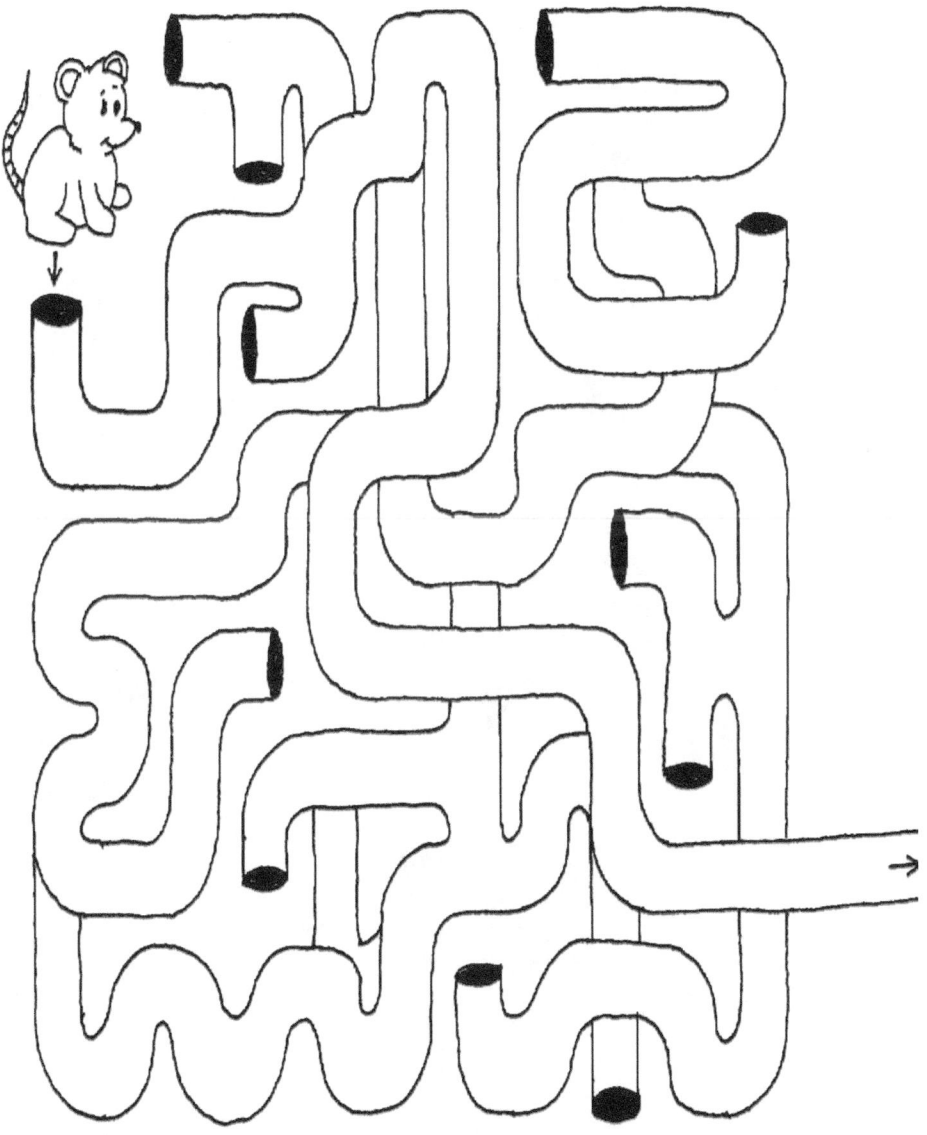

Brian has been lifted up by his three balloons.
If he wants to get on the ground, he has to climb
down between the other balloons.
Mark his way!

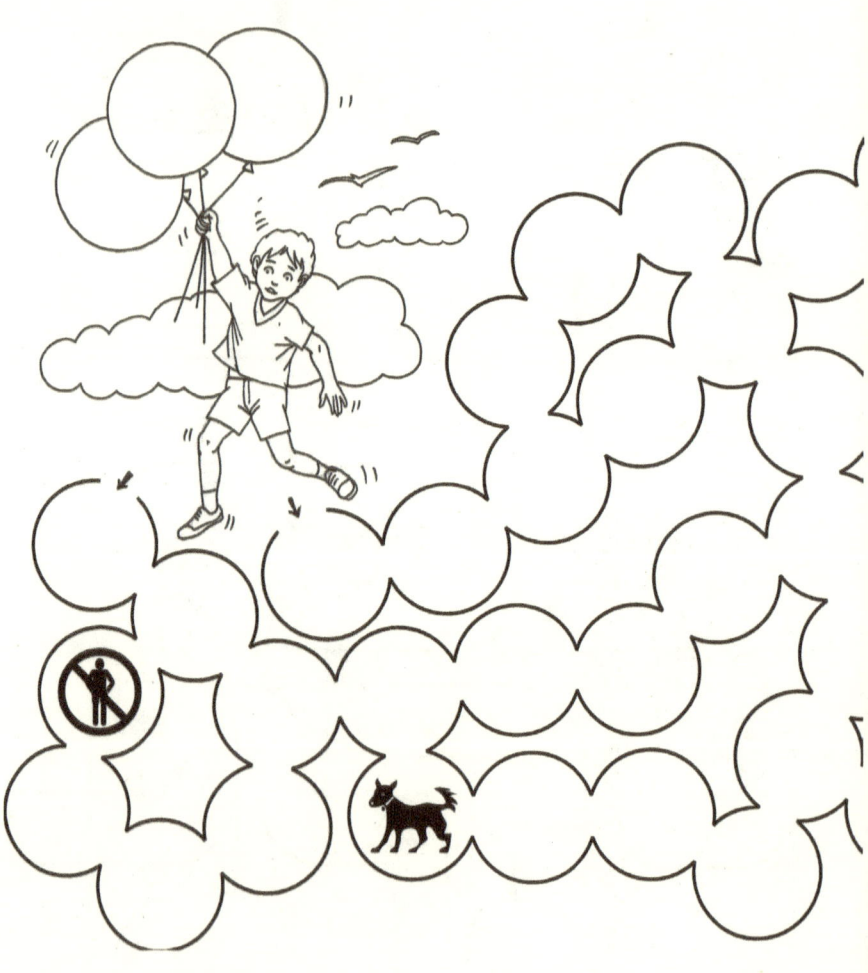

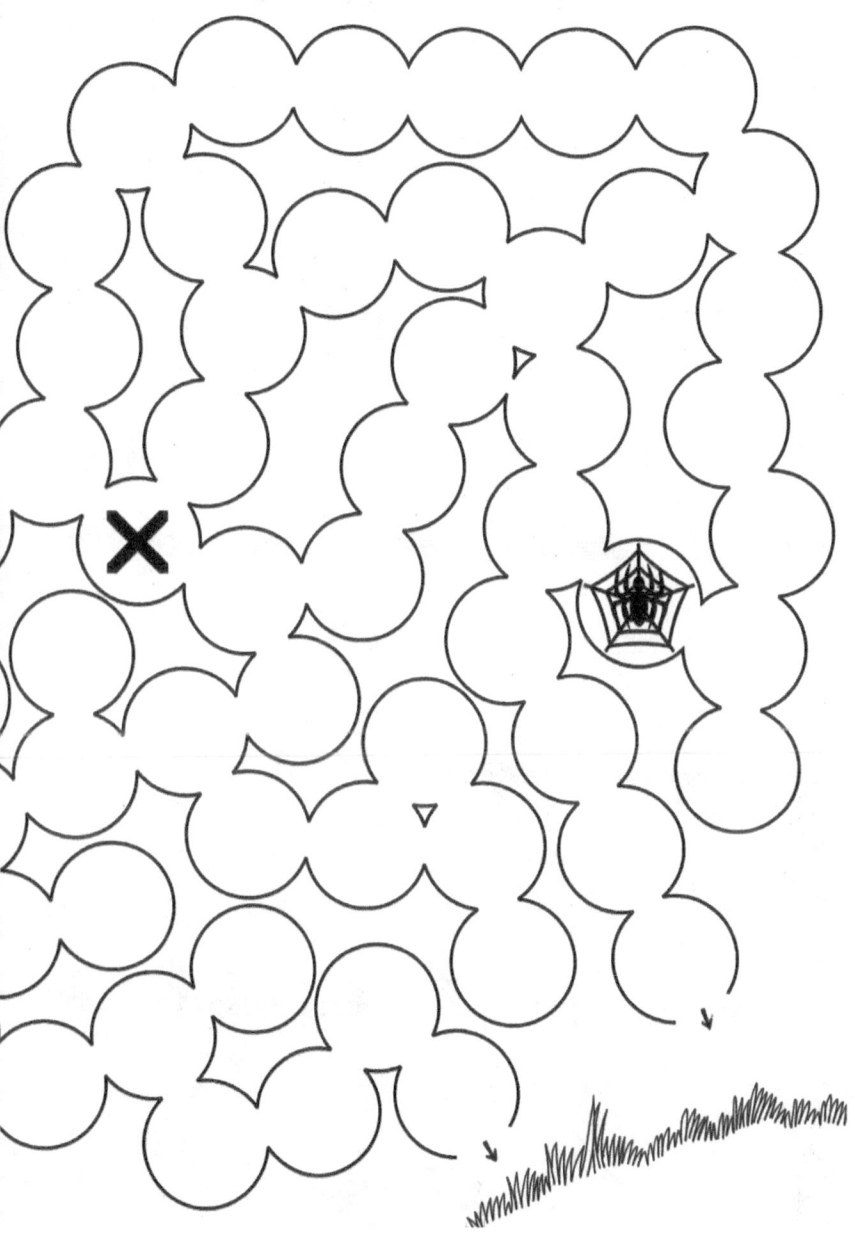

The little goldfish has been captured by fishermen.
Help him to escape from the net!
Mark!

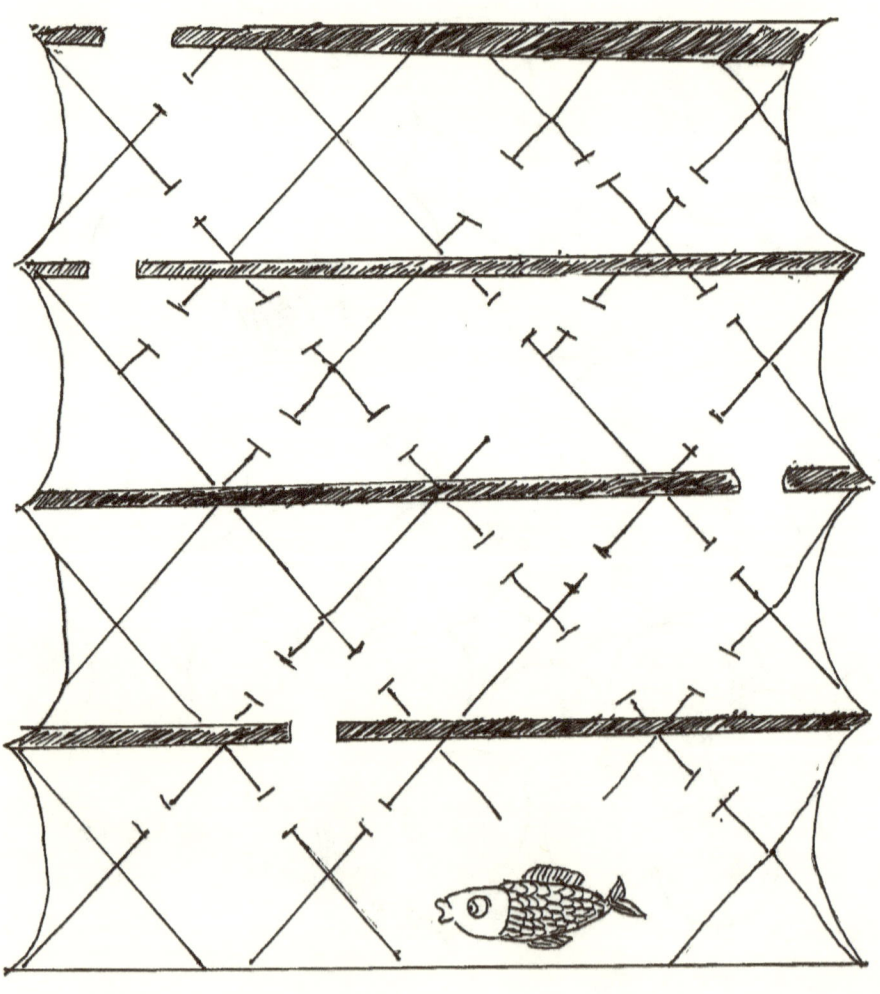

The fox would like to move to a new house.
Lead him to his new house and mark his way!

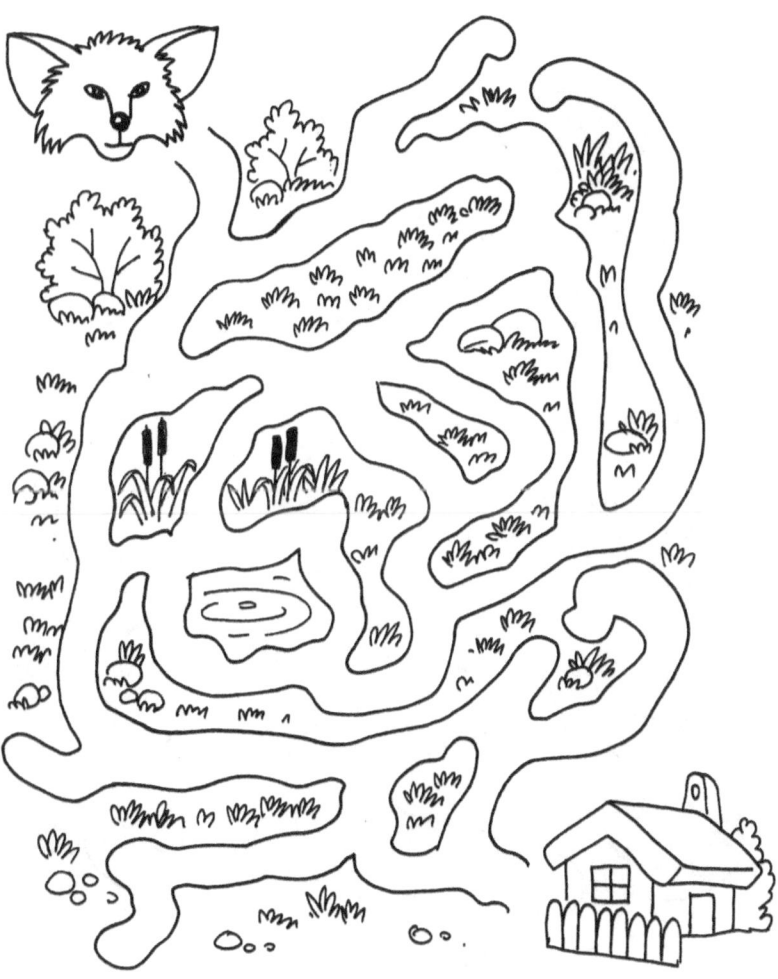

Help the prince to get in the palace, so
he can find the princess.
Mark his way!

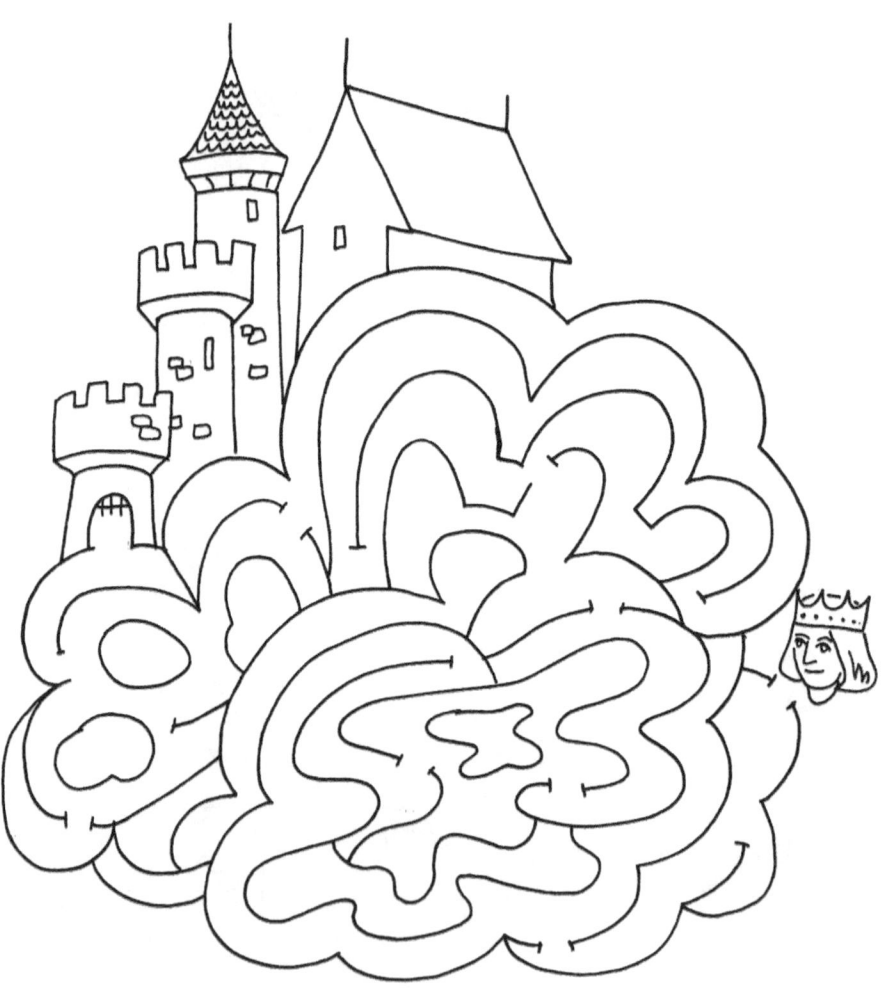

www.ingramcontent.com/pod-product-compliance
Lightning Source LLC
Chambersburg PA
CBHW021931170526
45157CB00005B/2281